A Short Life of Saint Francis

By
JOSEPH BERNHART

Translated by
MATTHEW J. O'CONNELL

FRANCISCAN HERALD PRESS
Chicago, Illinois 60609

ii

A Short Life of Saint Francis, by Joseph Bernhart, translated by Matthew J. O'Connell from the German *Franz von Assisi, Leben und Wort: Antwort des Christlichen Herzens,* published in 1935 and 1947 by Caritas-Verlag, Freiburg im Breisgau, Germany. Copyright © 1977 by Franciscan Herald Press, 1434 West 51st Street, Chicago, Illinois 60609. All rights reserved.

Library of Congress Cataloging in Publication Data:
Bernhart, Joseph, 1881-1969.
    A short life of Saint Francis.

    Translation of Franz von Assisi, Leben und Wort.
    1. Francesco d'Assisi, Saint, 1182-1226.
2. Christian saints—Italy—Assisi—Biography.
3. Assisi—Biography. I. Title.
BX4700.F6B4813   271'.3'024   77-6702
ISBN 0-8199-0675-1

NIHIL OBSTAT:
    Mark Hegener O.F.M.
        Censor Deputatus

IMPRIMATUR:
    Msgr. Richard A. Rosemeyer, J.D.
        Vicar General, Archdiocese of Chicago

April 4, 1977

MADE IN THE UNITED STATES OF AMERICA

FOREWORD

Some forty years ago Joseph Bernhart wrote and published an excellent short life of St. Francis under the title: *Franz von Assisi, Leben und Wort: Antwort des Christlichen Herzens (Francis of Assisi, Life and Words: Response of the Christian Heart)*. An English translation, by Matthew J. O'Connell, was published serially in *Franciscan Herald* during the year 1976 to commemorate the 750th anniversary of the death of St. Francis.

Joseph Bernhart, an eminent theologian and church historian, is best known in the United States for his outstanding work entitled *The Vatican as a World Power*, translated into English by George N. Schuster. His short life of St. Francis is likewise an outstanding delineation of the Poverello's character, saintliness, and influence. Even those who have read and reread longer biographies of the Little Poor Man of Assisi, will find this short life rewarding reading; and those who are looking for a short study of the real St. Francis, based on the sources but without numerous references and notes, will find none better than Bernhart's short life.

— THE PUBLISHER

CONTENTS

ILLUSTRATIONS

CHAPTER I

NEW KNIGHT OF CHRIST

WHEN FRANCIS CAME on the Assisi scene in 1182 as a son
of a rich cloth merchant, the world was the unholy place it
has always been. What he regarded as happiness in the
years of carefree youth could not long keep its hold on him.
The communes were awakening to a new self-awareness, and
an irrepressible vitality was asserting itself on every side,
but what civic virtue and the hard pursuit of gain were
amassing was hourly threatened by the ceaseless wars between the cities. The Umbrian countryside rarely knew the
repose of peace; raids, destruction, and atrocities fill the
pages of the chroniclers. Initially only threatened, not yet
badly shaken, by the rise of the middle class, the feudal system
retained its cultural importance and had more power than
anything else to grip the imagination even of a young man
so high on the social ladder as this Giovanni, whom his father
called "Francesco." The ancient conflict between Emperor
and Pope was a source of opposition with the religious unity
that bound these two parties together, and it gave rise to
factions in public life. Religious and knightly ideals were
blended in the Crusades. The Church determined the spirit
of the age as a whole, and its socio-religious character was
no obstacle to the formation of groups of like-minded people

who gathered under the banner of disparate slogans drawn from the treasury of tradition. Brotherhoods sprang up in great numbers, finding a model as well as a basis and support in the flourishing corporative life of the cities. As cultural life became more complex and independent, people adopted a more critical attitude to the clergy as the representatives of the Church and contrasted their outward lives and activity with the inner truth they were obligated to profess and follow.

At the papal court worldly men had gained control. Men who followed a stricter conscience rose in protest; among them were some who for the sake of their personal message lost sight of the Church as a whole. A man of this type, resembling in many respects the earlier schismatics, was Petrus Waldes, the "Poor Man of Lyons," as he was called, and founder of the Waldensians. He distributed his extensive wealth to the starving poor, and preached penance; but he also renewed the old puritan teaching, gave a heretical bent to the concept of poverty, and was finally condemned by Rome. The Albigensians were a greater danger to the age; led astray by the presence of evil in the world, they denied a single Providence governing all reality and preached a belief in two gods, one the good creator of the soul, the other the evil maker of the material world. The Church took extreme measures against these heretics, and bloody battles were fought to rescue the idea of the one supreme God. The Church and, with her, the peoples of the west felt their Christian foundations threatened by erroneous notions: that any good man is a priest, that the sacraments of the Church are to be disdained because the whole earth has been blessed, that every good man is God's son in the same sense as Christ.

In this stormy social and religious atmosphere, Francis grew up with little schooling in the things of the spirit and

reached the time of life when a man for the first time becomes a question to himself, yet will accept no answer from
anyone but himself.

Francis was vain, happy-go-lucky, foppish, always ready
for any bold enterprise; he liked to be different from others,
to set the tone, to be in the limelight; at bottom, he was
generous, sensitive, lovingly open to everything, and his ego
had countless ways of asserting itself.

Such, according to the accounts, was the life and character
of this slender, graceful, aristocratic youth. From this disparate material that nature provided, grace would be able to
fashion what it wanted. Or — did nature possess these ex-
cellences and defects because the perfection to come required
them? Does the ultimate goal guide the whole development in
man as it does in non-rational creatures?

Among the little city's elegant young people (*la jeunesse
dorée*) who formed a small group of devoted friends Francis
was the central figure in their unrestrained pursuit of pleasure.
His father's prosperity provided him with money to spend
lavishly. With his obscure intuition that he was called to
something special, he loved to strike poses and to celebrate
the festival of life by feasting with his companions. This
heart full of high spirits (precisely what the New Testament
means by *perisseuein*) was ever dreaming of the day when
he would be a great prince and honored by all. But, before
the dream came true — and it did come true in its own
fashion — he had to be laid low by a serious illness. A sweet
separation from the routine of everyday life left him without
desire and scornful of what he had become accustomed to;
it freed him from the bonds of carefree worldliness. Thus the
first blow was struck against the protective shell that sur-
rounded his soul.

But his dreams of a great future did not leave him as he

lay sick. In this golden age of knighthood, when the clanking
of tournies and jousting echoed throughout the land, when
celebrated troubadours from the love courts of Provence were
spreading their "gay science" across the land and traveling
ministrels sang the tales of Arthur and his Round Table, when
the military Orders and the Crusades formed a new and
strangely exhilarating ideal by fusing the warrior's sensual
pleasure in battle with pious Christan desire; in this age
when courtly love was regarded as the key to heaven and
earth, Francesco, a man of high aspiration, could not resist
the fascination of knighthood. He armed himself and joined
a fellow-citizen in his travels to the field of war in the south.
The day before his departure, while yet weaponless, he did
a knightly deed: gave his brand-new cloak to a poor knight.
This was the same chivalry (*courtoisie*) of the heart that
once, when he had turned a beggar away from his father's
busy shop, made him repent, run after the man, and give
him double his usual alms. But now, on the journey to Apulia
and his knighting, some obscure event stopped him in his
tracks. He had started out in the morning full of joy, after
a dream in the night had given him a glimpse of his future
glorious palace, but by evening, when he reached Spoleto,
his enthusiasm had died. Had his noble companion mocked
the merchant's son of lower rank and insulted him? Did
some movement in his own soul make him withdraw into
himself? We do not know.

That night he dreamed again and heard a conversation.
"Where are you bound for, Francis?" — "For Apulia, to
become a knight!" — "Who can bestow greater favor on
you, the master or the servant?" — "The master." — "Then,
why do you abandon the master for the servant, the superior
for the inferior?" — "Lord, what do you want me to do?" —
"Return home! I shall reveal to you the meaning of what

you have seen." Early next morning, he turned his horse's head toward home, his armor now like a strange and uncomfortable garment about him. (Cf. Leg. 3 Comp., 6 in *Omnibus of Sources*, p. 895.)

In Assisi he met mockery on every street. He wandered about for a few days like a real knight of sorrowful countenance, groping toward his new future and the different, unknown, unsuspected greatness that lay ahead. All the things of this world were dull and insipid: that was all he knew and all he needed to know to prevent him becoming either merchant or knight. His father raged at this fool of a son, and the people laughed at the dethroned king of Assisi's youth and called him a booby.

Not a knight by social class, yet knightly indeed through the gifts of nature and grace, but now become a question mark to himself — such was Francis during the next three years. He was already well over twenty, but he was in the tormenting position of a man who does not know which way to turn; he had cast the old aside, but only in obscure intuitions could he feel the new drawing near. He went joylessly to work in his father's business, but he took every opportunity to slip away and reconcile himself to the shadows that lie upon all human existence. On long walks into lonely places, often accompanied by a companion of his own age, he took counsel with himself; he would enter a cave and pray so fervently that he seemed to his friend's eye to be radiant with light.

He asked his new Lord to bestow on him the most precious knowledge of all, the knowledge men find it most difficult to attain: he asked him to make known his will, God's will, for this "new knight of Christ." His soul grew stronger through acts of extraordinary self-conquest. Once, as he rode through the countryside, deep in thought, he met a leper and with instinctive repugnance turned his horse aside. The next moment he remembered his great new resolutions and felt ashamed; dismounting, he gave the man an alms and kissed his hand, as people would kiss the hand of a priest. The smell of the lepers' huts repelled him from afar off, yet a few days later he sought out the lepers there in order to serve and care for them. He did not contract the disease, but he did win the freedom which mastery over his nature gave him and of which he would speak years later in his *Testament*. His conversion to the "way of repentance" had begun; soon he would leave "worldliness."

A farmer admonishes Francis to be as saintly as people thought he was.

CHAPTER II

MY LADY POVERTY

We MUST NOT overlook the young Francis' attraction to the striking and unusual and his desire for that special notice that is given to the outsider who lives his life apart and thus calls attention to himself as a critic of his age. Yet neither this trait of character nor the sympathy for the masses of oppressed people around him that deeply stirred his noble, compassionate nature can adequately explain his future course. In his case, as in that of any saint, we cannot expect a satisfactory explanation from psychology. In any development of the physical or mental order the complete end result is present from the beginning as the goal to be achieved, even if it be hidden from the being who is moving toward it. The essential form of a plant must exist prior to the seed, since all growth proceeds from and toward that form. In the world of freedom too, that is, in man, the starting point is a primordial ordination toward a divinely predetermined final state which man, precisely because he is free, can reach or fail to reach. To reach it requires a prompt obedience and openness to a transcendent power without whose help man cannot attain his own fulfillment, because his nature is not whole and will, if left to itself, always be something unfinished. Here we have the basic condition for every complete development of the person who has once grasped what "being a Christian" means and who, knowing it, devotes all his energies to becoming it.

This attitude of readiness, which has been given the deeply meaningful name of "obediential potency" (*potentia oboedientialis*), this power of obedience to the creator by which we put our nature at his disposal so that he may transform and elevate it through supernatural grace, gives Christian life in its entirety the character of a response. The Christian answers a call which he hears within himself but cannot regard as a merely natural or inherent factor in his interior world. In fact, so little does he think it merely natural, that he can put up with the fearful tensions generated between his native self and this attraction which is often alien and does violence to him; he can submit to it to the very end, though this end may itself be extremely painful. The Christian thus lives in fidelity to a second "self" and acts among men with the unshakable conviction that the Lord of history is acting in and through him in accordance with his own good, even if stern, law. Not even the saint himself, much less his astonished or perhaps even scornful fellow men, can assign meaning and order to each stage of his development. But the time will come, if not for the saint himself, then for the world as it looks back, when the confused threads of deed and destiny show themselves to make up a tapestry with a design and inner law of its own.

We do not know of many incidents from the years of Francis' interior formation. Those we do know, however, are the ones that caught the attention of his contemporaries and often affected them deeply because the incidents were so vivid and so drastic in character. These outward actions allow us to infer decisive interior moments in Francis' growing alienation from the "world" (*saeculum*) and from the way in which

many even of those who intended to be Christians adapted to
the demands of that world.

Once again, after his dreams of knighthood had collapsed,
Francis invited his friends to his still popular table, though
he did so with some misgivings. When they had feasted, his
friends strolled through the streets singing from midnight to
dawn the carefree songs of revellers. Francis stayed behind,
thinking, motionless as though turned to stone — "What's
the matter with you? Are you thinking of marrying?" —
"Yes! I have a bride so noble, rich ,and beautiful that you
have never seen her like!" Cf. Leg. 3 Comp., 7 in *Omnibus
of Sources* p. 896.)

With these words his betrothal to Lady Poverty began. She
was more than a concept or an ideal; she was a compelling
figure that stood in his path; she was almost a person, and
real enough to elicit from him this promise of fidelity. This
was how the ancients had experienced the approach of their
gods, and how Petrarch, a century after Francis, would feel
Melancholy entering his chamber. Francis' plastic imagination
was not here personifying a passing impulse of the heart;
rather, an elemental force took possession of him and he had
to reckon with it from this point. He now had a betrothed;
he would be faithful to her to the best of his ability and
would always refer to her as "My Lady Poverty" (*domina
mea Paupertas*).

A firm decision has been made (Dante: *sua dura inten-
zione*); equally firm and unconditioned would be the future
decisions of this follower of him who gave himself most un-
conditionally. All that was tender and pliant in his nature, all
that sought an outlet in the feelings of love he poured out
on others, did not weaken the hard bedrock from which these
decisions sprang. Unfortunately, this face with the thin, chis-
elled lips of the man of decision, and this character which,

like that of anyone who influences generations of men, has its terrifying aspect have, in the memory of posterity, been softened, rendered childish, and thus falsified. The result has been the Poverello and his perpetual sunshine. Yet how his black eyes must have kindled every time a new act of "the foolishness of the cross" liberated him a little more from the bonds of the old self!

As Francis was increasingly repelled by the world in which the lust for possessions and appearances was everything, his ears became more finely attuned to the call that reached him from that other world in which dire poverty and suffering were the norm. Prayer in chapels apart, prostrations before the scourged Man on the Cross, and all the other acts of external piety could not quench his thirst for a new way of life. The Crucified Christ wants men who will follow his word and example; he wants mercy. Francis therefore began to give, and to give with a generous hand. On a pilgrimage to Rome he like the others threw some of his money on the tombs of the Apostles, and ended up throwing it all away on the floor of the churches. But was even that enough? Was it not still only a part of his possessions, only the alms that rich men give? No, it was not enough simply to give to beggars: he must himself become a beggar and extend his hand for a paltry coin. That was the kind of poverty he wanted. And so, like the other wretches, he, the son of rich Bernardone, crouched on the steps of St. Peter's and learned what it was to beg.

At home, he took some pieces of goods and went off to another city where he sold both goods and horse. The money gained he intended to give to the poor priest at San Damiano, his beloved place of prayer, so that he might keep it and support himself with it in his customary frugal style. The priest refused the money, however; perhaps he was also rejecting

the plans of this intense son of the middle class with his anti-
bourgeois rebelliousness. He certainly knew Francis from
the latter's many visits to the dilapidated little church, and
he had already accepted money to buy oil for the lamp Francis wished to keep burning before the crucifix that had been
witness to the enlightenment granted to him on many occasions as he prayed before it. This time, however, although the
priest was willing to let Francis stay in the church, he rejected
the big bag of money. Francis threw it down on a windowsill
and remained within the beloved walls of the church. But
his father, who finally learned the truth after long inquiry,
unleashed a storm of rage on the head of his good-for-nothing
son. Francis heard of his father's anger and, still fearing an
open conflict, fled and hid for a week in a cave where he lived
on the supplies brought him by a servant who was in on the
secret. After a difficult inner struggle and much tearful prayer
that the Lord might rescue him from persecution, the shell
of the nut cracked open and his heart was liberated. Ablaze
with joy and jubilation, he went up to Assisi to confront the
oppressor. In the public square, a crowd set upon the ragged,
emaciated son of Bernardone and followed him home with
curses, mud, and stones.

When the wild scene of the meeting with his father had
been played out, Francis was locked in a dark room, his hands
chained. Bernardone then went off on a business trip, and
Francis' mother released her imprisoned son, but no persua-
sion by this woman who wanted peace in her family could
keep him from returning to San Damiano. The inner force
that drove him also confirmed the truth of a decisive experience which Francis had in this church, according to his biographer. From a crucifix depicting the Son of God in grave
yet gentle majesty Francis heard a voice telling him he should
build up the Lord's house that was falling into ruin. Startled

and trembling, Francis replied: "I will do it gladly, Lord!"
(Cf. Leg. 3 Comp., 13 in *Omnibus of Sources,* p. 903.) The
command and the promise, first taken literally, later understood in a higher sense as referring to the renewal of Christ's
Church that had become too worldly, bound Francis irresistibly to this spot.

When the elder Bernardone returned, he sharply rebuked
his wife. In vain, however, did he visit his son in his hermitage and try with threats to persuade him that, being a disgrace to his family, he should at least depart from his native
city. The father met only stubborn resistance; he therefore
brought suit against his son so that he might at least recover
the price of the goods and the horse. In view of his new state
as a hermit, Francis challenged the competence of the secular court; he would now be subject only to the spiritual authority. The city fathers were not at all averse to withdrawing
from an awkward situation, and Bernardone went to the
bishop. The latter summoned the debtor and told him he had
acted wrongly and must give back the money .The money was
easily recovered, for it still lay on the window sill where Francis had thrown it.

The day of restitution that now followed is memorable in
the history fo the conflict, always tragic in character, between
the two laws that present claims, each of them rightly, to the
fully mature human being. The law of the heart, which the
son wished to obey, was in this case defeated from the very
beginning by the law governing bourgeois society, as the
father — not unjustly, yet as a man incapable of the higher
justice which his son represented — demanded back what belonged to him. In the open air, before the Cathedral of San
Rufino, the bishop sat as judge between the two men and re-
peated his order to the defendant. It was as though a whirl-
wind were descending on Francis and darkening heaven and

earth for him. He satisfied the claim and even went beyond it with a sarcasm worthy of the Bible: "Lord, I gladly give it back; in fact, not only the money but my clothing as well!" He ran into the bishop's palace and stripped himself, removing even the hairshirt he was wearing. Naked he had been born to his father; naked, he would now depart from him! He returned outside to the crowd and laid money and clothing at the bishop's feet. "Listen to me, everyone! From now on I am a servant of the Lord. I am giving back to that man there not only his money but all the clothing I have received from him. Now I can freely say, not 'Peter Bernardone, my father!', but 'Our Father, who art in heaven!'" The bonds of blood and family were broken. Father and son were each satisfied in their passion for the good in which they found happiness; each was victor in the conflict. But the father, shamed and enraged, carried his wretched money back home, while the bishop, struggling to hold back his tears, embraced the naked man and covered him with his cloak.

The birthday of the Child Jesus Francis observed with inexpressible eagerness over all other feasts, saying that it was the feast of feasts, on which God, having become a tiny infant, clung to human breasts. — Who can express, who can understand how far Francis was from glorying in anything save in the Cross of our Lord? — With a love that came from his whole being, Francis burned for the Sacrament of the Lord's Body; and he was carried away with wonder at the loving condescension and the most condescending love shown there. Not to hear at least one Mass each day, if he could be there, he considered no small contempt. — Celano, **Second Life,** 151, 154, 152, in **Omnibus of Sources,** pp. 521-524.

CHAPTER III

THE KING'S HERALD

THE SIGNIFICANT GESTURE of standing before the bishop to renounce his earthly father and embrace his Father in heaven put a seal of confirmation on Francis' conversion (*metanoia*), which one biographer calls the *ordo versus* or life based on a reversal of a man's whole view of the world. The new life was hard on the homeless Francis. Indeed, his perseverance through the terribly harsh two or three years that followed, years that ground him down in body and spirit, was a miracle of perseverance and sufficient proof that his mission, though ing this laughing-stock of a son whom he had loved with such fatherly tenderness. Francis could not listen to these curses without being moved, but he gave expression to his emotion in a way no one else could have thought of. At the price of some of the food he had begged, he got another beggar to act as his father: "When you see my father cursing me, and I say to you, 'Bless me, father,' you sign me with the cross and bless me in his place." Thus it happened, and Bernardone had to submit to a lesson from his son: "Do you not realize that God can give me a father whose blessing will counter your curses?" (Cf. Leg. 3 Comp., 23 in *Omnibus of Sources*, p. 913.)

By all accounts, public opinion concerning the beggar's

seriousness and tenacity began to change, but his family could not get over the blow to their reputation. Even Francis' younger brother, Angelo, poured out bitter scorn on him. One winter morning, as Angelo and a friend passed the shabbily dressed Francis who was lost in prayer, Angelo said to his companion: "Go and ask him to sell you a penny's worth of his sweat." Francis heard him and replied in French: "No, I prefer to sell it to my Lord — at a higher price." (Cf. Leg. 3 Comp., 24 in *Omnibus of Sources*, p. 913.)

The rebuilding of San Damiano was finally completed, but Francis also wanted lamps to be kept burning there continually. One day, as he was begging for oil, he came to a house where sounds of play and entertainment met him. He suddenly felt ashamed and discouraged, probably at the thought that some of his former companions were there, and so he passed the house by. Was not all he was doing just nonsense? The earlier years when he had lived as a man among men rose up to reproach him for the rootless existence in which he had now entangled himself. It was one of those moments that lie in wait for men dedicated to God as they go their way in solitude of heart. Can something really be God's will if everyone else calls it freakishness? And yet, "whoever puts his hand to the plow but keeps looking back is unfit for the reign of God" (Lk 9:62). Thus the irresolute Francis found within himself a deeper reason for shame than the fact that he must beg. Filled with consolation, he entered the house, confessed his weakness to all present, and in a new spirit of freedom collected alms from them.

After he had renovated another church near Assisi, he turned his loving attention to the old country chapel dedicated to Our Lady of the Angels; it belonged to the Benedictines of Subasio and lay below Assisi but further out in the plain. It had long been dear to him, and he had once been seen weeping there over the suffering of Christ. Henceforth, Portiuncula, as its owners called it, would indeed be his little portion of earth and the focus of a life that gradually developed and made its presence felt over wide stretches of time and space. After putting the place in good repair as an act of veneration to the Mother of God and the angels, Francis experienced here the decisive enlightenment concerning his vocation.

On the morning of February 24, 1208, the feast of St. Matthias, Francis was serving Mass for a monk from Subasio. (His writings make evident to us the deep interior devotion he had always had to the Eucharistic mystery.) On this particular day the Gospel was from the tenth chapter of St. Matthew's Gospel:

"As you go, make this announcement: "The reign of God is at hand!" Cure the sick, raise the dead, heal the leprous, expel demons. The gift you have received, give as a gift. Provide yourselves with neither gold nor silver nor copper in your belts; no traveling bag, no change of shirt, no sandals, no walking staff. The workman, after all, is worth his keep.

"Look for a worthy person in every town or village you still obscure to him and only gradually acquiring some clear contours, was of superhuman origin. But, now that the Lord of the Gospel had laid hold of him, he had no desire to kick against the goad. His thoughts were all of how he in turn could lay hold of the world for his Lord.

The time was the year 1207; snow still lay on Mt. Subasio. Through its woods and through the whole countryside around Assisi Francis wandered, sometimes singing ballads (in the French language he loved) in praise of fidelity to his liege lord. His clothing was a shabby garment given him by a servant of the bishop on that fateful day; on the back of his cloak, ever since the day of the trial, was a cross, smeared on with plaster, as a sign of the Lord to whose service he was dedicated.

Once, on the way to Gubbio, hunger and cold drove him to become a kitchen-boy in a monastery, but after a few days they sent the unknown vagabond on his way again. As he went on toward Gubbio, some tramps suddenly emerged from the woods and seized him. "Who are you?" — "I am the herald of the great King. What is that to you?" They saw there was nothing to take from this poor fool, so they threw him into a ditch still filled with April snow: "You clown! You 'herald of God'! Lie there!" Francis climbed painfully out, but his heart rejoiced. (Cf. Cel. I, 16, in *Omnibus of Sources*, p. 242.)

At his friend's house in Gubbio he was given the hermit's garb he wanted: a knee-length outer garment, a rope for a belt, sandals, and a penitent's staff. He stayed at a hospital with the lepers, washing them, changing their bandages, and sometimes, in complete self-forgetfullness, even kissing their sores.

Next, he returned to San Damiano, in order to carry out his commission from the crucified Saviour. How was he to do it? He had his two hands, but no stone, no lime, and no money to buy these and other supplies. He went up to the city and attracted people's attention by singing ballads; after each song, he begged of them: "Give me one stone and you will have a reward in heaven; two stones, a double reward; three stones, a triple reward!" Some laughed at him; others had to fight back their tears as they thought of the marvelous changes that occurred in men's lives. Francis collected the stones he had been given and carried them on his slender shoulders to the church. (Cf. Leg. 3 Comp., 21 in *Omnibus of Sources*, p. 911).

The priest's remaining doubts about Francis' seriousness in

serving God now disappeared, and he provided him with richer and more nourishing food. Francis, who was now both stone-carrier and mason, wanted nothing more than a couple of helpers, but when he sat down in the evening he found before him a well-laid table. He soon grew scrupulous about it and thought to himself as he prayed: "Do you think you will find, everywhere you go, such a kind-hearted priest? This is not the life of the poor that you chose for yourself." (Cf. Leg. 3 Comp., 22 in *Omnibus of Sources,* p. 912.)

The next day, therefore, he took a beggar's bag and went into the city to beg not only for oil and candles for the church, but also for food for his bowl. He had been accustomed from childhood to delicate, tasty food, and so in the beginning he had to force down the mess in his bowl. But he overcame himself, as had done the first time he kissed a leper, and since in every onslaught on his nature he was guided by spiritual motives, especially that of following the suffering Lord, he inured his carnal self in an astonishing degree to a very severe discipline. He suffered no harm from this; on the contrary, it was with heightened energies that he would at last be able to thank the Lord for turning the first movements of fleshly rebellion into a feeling of well-being.

When his father met him out begging, the purseproud merchant who also set great store by the respect of others was overcome by shame and wrath and could not keep from curscome to and stay with him until you leave. As you enter his home bless it. If the home is deserving, your blessing will descend upon it. If it is not, your blessing will return to you. If anyone does not receive you or listen to what you have to say, leave that house or town, and once outside it shake its dust from your feet" (Mt. 10:7-14).

Now his mind was filled with light; the Lord had spoken to him for the second time. After Mass, when the priest at his request had given him a more detailed explanation of the words, he was overwhelmed with the joy the Holy Spirit gives: "That is what I wish and seek!" (Cf. Cel. I, 22 in *Omnibus of Sources,* p. 247.) — What was it the Lord was urging upon him? Complete poverty; itinerant preaching of the rule of God that would cause a radical change in the world; and bringing the peace of Jesus Christ to city and countryside.

Without further reflection, this true doer of the Word set to work. In holy simplicity he did what was immediately possible for him by changing his garb. We who look back from a different age should not regard this action as less important than Francis did. In it he shows not only the childlike eye of the southerner for the importance of accidentals nor only his special talent for giving sensible expression to spiritual states and experiences, but also medieval man's basic tendency to see visible things as signs. Francis' action shows a poetic relation to reality, and, as we shall see, it is essential that we understand this relation if we are properly to empathize with the person and activity of our Saint. Immediately, then, he applied the Lord's missionary discourse in a literal way by getting rid of sandals, staff, and traveling bag, contenting himself with a single shirt which he tied around him with a cord instead of a belt, and renouncing all money. Now, having openly and unreservedly taken apostolic poverty for his bride, he set about doing apostolic work.

CHAPTER IV

THIS IS OUR LIFE

A BRIEF LOOK at the situation in the High Middle Ages of the Hohenstaufen period will enable us to gauge at its proper value the courage of Francis, this "fool in the world's eyes," as he haled his age before the judgment-seat of the Gospel. Francis was a man of limited education and probably had little interest in politics, and so he set about his work without much reflection on the society of his time. His mission was to be a young David going out against Goliath. In his heart he had received light from on high as to what he should do, and the power of this inner impulse made planning and consideration of favorable and unfavorable circumstances quite unnecessary. Francis had the eye which, according to Scripture, causes the whole body to be full of light. Consequently, he could see, from the snares laid by the Evil One within his own narrow circle, how men were set against the Lord's manifest will, and could gather from his experience of this little work how the world at large lay under the power of evil. The bitter aftertaste left by his earlier life of pleasure taught him, now that the cross had become for him the standard of human existence, what man is when left to his own resources and what he must become if he is to satisfy his Creator and Redeemer.

Ploremus ante Dominum qui fecit nos: in the presence of
the Lord who made us, let us shed the tears that spring from
knowledge of who we are and what our guilt is. After becoming a penitent and discovering to his great joy the power
of penance to heal, renew, and give true life, Francis cried
out to the whole world and invited it to enter that kingdom
which is like a wedding banquet. Who would enter   Only
those brought in from the hedges and byroads?

Despite the sad condition of Empire, State, and Church,
the name "Christendom" was still rightly applied at this
period because the relationship of the world and men to Christ
as their Redeemer was still accepted as the all-embracing
norm of life. The conflicts between the spiritual and the secular powers were not caused by opposing views on the kingdom
of God as the ultimate source of meaning for all that makes up
human history. It was another question entirely, of course,
whether the moral state of men corresponded to the demands
of God's rule as explained in its basic text, the Gospel. Everyone knew how greatly the worst kind of worldliness had cor-
rupted even the Church. Pope Innocent III, to whom Francis
would present his great undertaking, went so far as to say
that all evil had its origin in the clergy.

At the same time, however, in the realm of thought and
belief (which is the source of spirituality) there was a great
deal of opposition to the treasure of truth preserved in the
Church of Christ. Even more dangerous than all the confus
ing heresies was the skepticism that turned a cold shoulder
to religion. The shadows of unbelief, sometimes barely notice-
able, sometimes very dark, drift like ghosts through the writings of the early thirteenth century; for evidence we need
only point to the love poetry and epics of the French and
Germans. The fear of some contemporaries that antichrist was
at the door becomes understandable if we set these signs of

breakdown in the old solid Christian unity alongside the social ills of Francis' time, the open tyranny which money exercised in the marketplace, the towns, and the Roman Curia, the conspicuous consumption of the higher clergy, and the forgetfulness of duty among the lower clergy.

In the divine plan that governs the history of mankind a little band of chosen men is sent from time to time to battle the Evil One and to bring rescue and healing. As prophets, apostles, or saints they speak to their age in God's name by speaking against it. Their vocation is the most difficult that can be imposed on men, because the world they are to win for the Lord desires nothing less than service under his banner. The more faithful these men are to the words and inspiration of their principal, the more unrest and upheaval they cause. They are working for the promised "unshakable kingdom" (Heb. 12:28) which shakes the inconstant created world to its foundations so that it may be remade into an unshakable kingdom that lasts forever.

How foolish, then to "explain" the messengers of Christ's kingdom "in terms of their age," and to equate the Church's saints with the other great men of history! *Deus mirabilis in sanctis suis.* But if God shows himself wonderful in his saints, they themselves inevitably escape our grasp and refuse to abide by our purely naturalistic explanations of them. Just as the Church of the Old and New Covenants has since the fall of man had its own proper history as the agent of God's ongoing work of salvation, so too the saint (in the distinctive sense given this term in the Church of the new covenant) has his proper history as a special instrument for convincing the world of the glory of Christ. By his own personal sanctification, which results from the cooperation of free will and grace, the saint begins, here in time, to body forth in his life and activity the claim of Christ to lordship over the world and to make that claim effective by means of his own special powers and gifts. He lays hold of, or rather is himself laid hold of by, one or other aspect of the Gospel command to become perfect, and, in public or in private, wittingly or unwittingly, he works in accordance with the intentions and by the power of the Spirit who remains with the Church "until the end of time" in order to bear "witness" to Christ and lead the Church "to all truth" (cf. Jn. 15:26; 16:13). The saint is, above all, the bearer of God's witness to himself in the history of the Church, and to the extent that, in the Lord's words, he "does the truth" (Jn. 3:21), he contributes to a deeper knowledge of that truth by himself and others.

Consequently, the history of a saint as such, if it is to be rightly understood, must not be separated from the history of the Church as such. This fact does not make it unnecessary, but on the contrary calls up on us, to ascertain, as accurately as we can, the character of the man, the influence of his times upon him, and the historical circumstances in which he travelled the road of holiness and came to "rule with Christ" (regnare cum Christo). For, according to Scripture, each person is called "by name," "star differs from star in glory" (1 Cor. 15:41), and "there is an appointed time for everything" (Eccl. 3:1), while "the heart of the wise man knows the right time and the right answer."

This man who surrendered everything in order to gain the field that contained the hidden treasure of the kingdom knew that he was called upon to obtain that treasure for others as well as himself. His biographers tell us that he took as his own the mission of preaching peace and conversion. Soon he came upon a few people — and many were to come after them — to whom he could say with Paul: "You became imitators of us and of the Lord, receiving the word despite great trials, with the joy that comes from the Holy Spirit" (1 Thes. 1:6).

His greatest influence was due to his example, for "the kingdom of God does not consist in talk but in power" (1 Cor. 4:20). Everytime he went up from Portiuncula to Assisi, and wherever he found listeners — in the open fields, in the streets, in people's homes — he spoke his simple brief summons to conversion of the world-entangled spirit, to self-forgetfulness, and especially to peace, the treasure he saw everywhere disappearing from the hearts of men and the human community.

The very thing he had become to the accompaniment of his fellow-citizens' laughter, namely, a fool of the cross, now lent power to his words and enabled men to see from his call to repentance that the rule of God was no laughing matter. Within a few days in April, 1209, Francis won his first companions, or rather, to use his words, the Lord gave these men to him as brothers.

First and foremost there was Bernard of Quintavalle, a rich young merchant who had observed from a distance the strange transformation of this contemporary with whom he was somewhat acquainted. Bernard went secretly to Portiuncula and asked Francis to visit him at night, and the conversation with this new Nicodemus did take place, unobserved, in Assisi. Bernard asked what he should do with his possessions, since he no longer wanted to keep them — Give them back to the Lord from whom he had received them. — How could this best be done? Francis was of the opinion that in such a perplexing situation one should ask the Lord himself for guidance.

The question was put to the Lord one morning in the nearby Church of San Nicolo, in the presence of another person, Peter of Catania, who was of the same mind as Bernard. They wished to learn from the book of the Gospels what instruction the Lord gave his disciples when he told them to renounce the world. Being but simple men, however, they could not find the passage, and so they asked the Lord to make his will known to them when they opened the book. Kneeling at the altar, Francis then took the book and opened it. His eye fell on the words: "If you seek perfection, go, sell your possessions, and give to the poor. . . ." (Mt. 19:21). He opened the book a second time and read: "Take nothing for the journey. . . ." (Lk. 9:3). And a third time: "If a man wishes to come after me, he must deny his very self, take up his cross, and begin to follow in my footsteps" (Mt. 16:24).

"Brothers," said Francis, "this is our life and rule!" Immediately the new companions sold their possessions and gave the proceeds to the poor; they clad themselves like Franis and began their life together at Portiuncula. Shortly after, others joined them. An elderly priest named Sylvester had looked on enviously as the companions gave their money to the poor, with Francis standing by in silent, joyous praise of God. He accused Francis of not having paid him enough for stones for San Damiano. Francis stuck his hand into Bernard's bag of money a couple of times and gave Sylvester handfuls of it as though it were sand or gravel. "Is that enough, master priest?" "Quite enough, brother!" said Sylvester and went home pleased. But then the whole business began to bother him, and he too became a follower. (Cf. Leg. 3 Comp., 29-30 in *Omnibus of Sources,* pp. 918-919.)

Before this, young Giles had already joined Francis, moved by the much talked of flight of Bernard and Peter from the world. Giles sought out Francis at Portiuncula, where he met him as he was coming from solitary prayer in the woods; on his knees Giles made his request. Francis praised the decision of this new knight of Christ. He took Giles first to the chapel, then to the other brothers, and introduced him to them: "The Lord has given us another good brother. Let us rejoice and eat together in love!" After the meal, Francis went up to Assisi with Giles, to see to the garments he needed. A poor woman asked an alms of them. Francis thought for a moment, and then his face lit up: "Let us give her cloak out of love for God!" Giles removed his cloak and gave it to her with a feeling of joy he would never forget. (Cf. Mirror of Perfection, 36 in *Omnibus of Sources,* p. 1162.) He always remained very close to his master. He undoubtedly had to pass through the dark wrestlings of the spirit, but these alternated with periods of luminous contemplation. We have plenty of testimony to show for many decades this willing servant contributed to the saint's work.

St. Francis dictates a Letter to All the Faithful.

This is a reminder, admonition, exhortation, and my testament which I, Brother Francis, worthless as I am, leave to you, my brothers, that we may observe in a more Catholic way the Rule we have promised to God. And may whoever observes this be filled in heaven with the blessing of the most high Father, and on earth with that of his most beloved Son, together with the Holy Spirit, the Comforter, and all the powers of heaven and all the saints. And I, Brother Francis, your poor worthless servant, add my share internally and externally to that most holy blessing. — **Writings** in **Omnibus of Sources,** pp. 69-70.

CHAPTER V

THE IDEAL OF THE GOSPEL

THE NEW BROTHERHOOD of six began to go out on preaching tours, where their sermons consisted of simple short exhortations to the basic commandments of the Gospel. The accounts of these early days are permeated by a spirit of ethereal joy, but they do not hide the difficulties attendant upon all beginnings. In fact, the success of the brothers was more like failure, for the barefooted beggars met with mockery or anger, matrons and young women fled from them, and the call to repentance, conversion, and poverty of spirit entered few ears, much less hearts. It was rarely that a listener said to himself: "If these men are not fools or drunkards, then they are perfect followers of the Lord." (Cf. Leg. 3 Comp., 34 in *Omnibus of Sources*, p. 922.)

All the more wonderful, then, was the firmness with which they kept to their chosen way of life. The corruption they saw everywhere on their journeys — the worship of mammon, the pauperization, the lust for power, the destructiveness — set them more than ever on fire for the message of God's rule, but it took a higher motivation than the ills of society to make them preachers in the wilderness, men ready to make supreme sacrifices for Gods' kingdom. Their perseverance is inexplicable apart from their faith, and their

faith apart from their prayer. Grace has its permanently valid
laws of operation, and the companions learned from experience the holy circle in which life is won through self-
surrender and leads in turn to a deeper, richer, more authen-
tic poverty of spirit. There were setbacks felt deep in the
heart, and hours of weariness, but stronger than all these was
the confidence Francis had that God had chosen him. At such
moments he could say to his brothers: "Be strengthened, dear
brothers, and rejoice in the Lord, and do not be sad because
you seem so few; and do not let either my simplicity or your
own dismay you, for, as it has been shown to me in truth by
the Lord, God will make us grow into a very great multi-
tude" (Cel. I, 27 in *Omnibus of Sources*, p. 250).

After Francis' first missionary journey to the March of Ancona, with Giles as his companion, three respected men of
Assisi asked for admission to the group; they too had distributed their goods to the poor. Once again, families were
up in arms, prospective heirs were disappointed, and other
parents were filled with concern that their sons too might
fall victim to the spiritual contagion of example. Defenders
of the bourgeois way of life condemned the stupidity of giving away one's property and living at the expense of others.
Even the secular and regular clergy were bitter about these
innovators who were casting suspicion not only on personal
property but even on the community-owned property of
the ancient religious Orders as though it were contrary to
the Gospel.

The displeasure of clerical and secular society had arguments to justify it. After all, property had always been protected by the Gospel, and without possessions held in common the immense good done by monasteries and religious
societies that followed the Rules of Augustine or Benedict
would have been impossible. Healthy common sense rebelled

against the new brotherhood, therefore, as did family feeling and the whole economic order of society, while the Church could not help thinking that the older poverty movements, which had degenerated into heresy or sectarianism, were now being followed by another that was open to the same dangers.

Inevitably, the life of the brothers became the subject of discussion between Francis and the bishop of Assisi, the closest person of authority in the Church. The bishop had long been well aware of people's worried objections to the brothers and their outbursts of feeling in public and private. In his abiding good will toward Francis he pointed out to him what was justified in people's reactions to the brotherhood. "Your way of life, possessing nothing in this world, seems to me very hard and difficult." (Cf. Leg. 3 Comp., 33 in *Omnibus of Sources,* p. 921.) But Francis was no longer a man of short-lived enthusiasm. His attack on worldliness, even in the Church, was grounded in a command from a higher source, and he could not refuse this command, alter it, or repudiate it as he could his own ideas and schemes. His loving nature had been deeply moved by God's love for man, and his noble soul challenged to respond freely to that love by loving men in imitation of God. He saw that such a response was impossible when the interlocking evils of money and power, power and money, held possession of men's souls. — "My Lord, if we had possessions, we would also need weapons to defend them. Then we would be caught up in the wretched disputes and lawsuits of our day that do so much harm to love of God and man. Therefore we wish to have no temporal possessions in this world." — Perhaps his answer refers even more clearly to the traffic in temporal goods that went on in the clerical world. The bishop, himself entangled in this traffic, could make no de-

cisive response to Francis' position and allowed him to
act as he saw fit.

Soon there would be even clearer evidence of what Francis thought of possessions and poverty, toil and begging. As
long as he continued to be in charge of the work he had
started, he allowed no business dealings and no accommoda-
tion to "reasonable practice" or the ways of this or that
spiritual organization. He did not say all must act as he did;
he conducted no zealous campaigns against possessions or
property. Far from it; he even warned his brothers on acca-
sion against railing at the happy children of plenty, for (he
said) God is their Lord, too, and can call them whenever he
wishes, and make them upright and holy. On the other hand,
no one should or could force him to own property. He fought
unyieldingly for this freedom of the Christian man, for in
his view poverty was indeed the ultimate and highest form
of freedom, the evangelical freedom to be at the disposal
of God, the Creator and Redeemer, in a love unhindered by
attachment to values of second or even lower rank. Poverty
for the sake of freedom meant more than a simple renunciation of possessions. It meant a full and unconditional trust
in God's guidance of the world and man. For that very reason,
in coming to grips with the realities of man's history, poverty renounced all material means of asserting itself and was
content simply to proclaim its own existence through living
example and the preached word. Where malice or power
barred the way, the evangelical law was to be obeyed: do
not return evil for evil.

Francis would push his way of life to that limit beyond
which man begins to tempt God. Unconditional reliance on
the unconditional God purified him of all utilitarianism but
also eliminated almost any consideration of that bridge between the world and God whose piers are nature and culture.
He allowed these values no place in himself and his work.

On the other hand, Francis did not attack them; rather, while himself keeping a good distance from them, he regarded them with mute respect. His loving nature was really capable of but one hatred: in his eyes, money and the power it exercises were the devil's work. But we would radically mistake Francis if we were to maintain that this prophet of poverty was motivated solely by such a hatred. No more than his divine Master did he think that a man could obey the command to love "with all your strength" merely by renouncing mammon. Love alone, which is the essence of God's rule on earth, roused and motivated him, drove him beyond the limits of his own nature, and even consumed him as fire consumes wood.

In Francis, as in hardly any other saint of the Middle Ages, mankind can see the critical decisions which the Gospel forces upon it when that Gospel is taken in its full and undiluted truth. In other words: Francis experienced the deep psychic distress of a man who is directly confronted by God but sees that, existing as he does among men and set over against God, he cannot be the kind of man whom the God revealed in Jesus Christ would have him be. In order to meet God's ideal of man, he would have to separate himself from the historical world, for as long as he is part of it he can never fulfill the commandment to be "perfect as your heavenly Father is perfect." Thus, behind the life of Francis, with its catalysmic upheavels and its staggering challenges, there looms up a great question: If we accept the Gospel view of reality, is it possible for man as man — that is, a being who is part of history and bound up with family and with a culture and its institutions — to live in such a way as to know that his life is also justified before the Lord of the Gospel? Can a person in this world be the kind of Christian and follower of Christ that will satisfy the Lord of heaven's kingdom, who alone can judge our true worth? — There is no point in evading the question or denying the unrest that has afflicted the world ever since the Son of God preached his good news. For, with Christ a "fire from heaven" came among us and nothing can extinguish it. Ever since the Messiah and his work gave their witness, the whole history of the saints has given proof of the unrest that is present in all men. Even in the birth-pangs of their own transformation and passage to a new kind of existence, the saints, whether they wanted to or not, have caused the men of their day to feel the same pangs, even when these saints were mocked or suffered as fools, persecuted as a source of scandal, or loved and honored as messengers of heaven.

But the Gospel exercises a destructive power only in the interests of preserving something more important. The Word became flesh in order that he might, in human form, definitively make man into the creature after God's image and might rescue this free being, who is part of history, for an eternal life above and subsequent to time. "To his own he came" in order to establish God's rule among all peoples. But his own, the people from whom he was born according to the flesh, did not accept him. They persecuted him and put him to death, so that the end of the Messiah-King and his failure among his own people took the form of a bloody sacrifice. Despite this outcome, his coming for man's sake did not lose its meaning and effectiveness, but henceforth the redemption of man would depend on the Cross and its acceptance. The suffering of the Word made flesh would also be the lot of others, most especially those of whom the Scriptures say: "Any who did accept him he empowered to become children of God. These are they who believe in his name" (Jn 1:12).

This second birth of man, who in it is begotten "by God,"

"from above," "by the Spirit," puts him on the path to glory but also brings him into the Messiah's kingdom of suffering. With the Messiah man reborn experiences pain and danger, temptation and persecution, and a rending of his natural and supernatural being to the point where he too suffers abandonment by God. But the meaning of all this is simply that this human being becomes a man after the fashion of the Word incarnate. For the Word became a man, and a suffering man, in order that those who accept and follow him as the suffering Messiah, may become truly his own, that is, men after the model of God's humanity, men divinized, or, in a word, children of God.

Thus, man and all that is human are turned topsy-turvy by the Gospel for their own good and their higher fulfillment. The Gospel tears down for the purpose of rebuilding; it destroys in order to produce something new that is worthy of God and man. In the language of the Gospel itself there is a transformation in which the new being cannot come into existence without a prior shattering and destruction, as is the case of the grain of wheat if it is to produce its fruit. But we would radically misconceive the transforming power of the Spirit if we thought of it as causing purely historical changes or simply altering the succession of temporal relationships. It is true enough that the material the Gospel works with exists in the here and now and that the field in which the seed of God's rule is to be sown exists in time and space. But the ultimate goal lies beyond time and earthly history. The kingdom of God as the Lord preaches it and his followers strive to make it a reality introduces a new dimension that eludes our natural powers yet is as real to faith as the natural world is, and in fact is more real than anything else The special distinctive thing that moves the Christian and forms the saint is that these men do not simply take that new dimension into account during their earthly lives, but approach everything else from its viewpoint, and viewpoint alone. They think and judge in the light of this dimension. They live in it with the firm conviction that "everything else" will be given to them. This accounts for their being strangers in a world that no one knows better than they do; for their attack on a world that no one loves more than they do; for their detachment from a world that no one joyfully experiences as God's creation as much as they do. It is written of St. Francis: "He loved to hear everything about him singing of his pilgrim existence in a foreign land."

The Church, as keeper of the Gospel, has, like the Gospel, a twofold duty in the service of a single goal. She must not stand in the way of the Gospel's transforming power, yet at the same time she must protect all things earthly, and especially man who is the center of all earthly things, from being destroyed in the name of the cross, even though God in his love for man sacrificed himself on that cross. According to the laws of God's kingdom which require both a separation from the world and a deeper involvement in the world — laws that are brought into perfect harmony only in the person of the eternal Lord of the kingdom — the Church must see to it that the energies of upheaval and transformation no less than those of peaceful maternal conservation continue to operate in her history, as long as both are justified by the Gospel. It is also her duty to protect the freedom of her children to serve the kingdom according to each ones' gifts, grace, and vocation. In this educational role as guardian of values, the Church's attention is directed to the words of Scripture: The spiritual man, who has the mind of Christ, can pass judgment on everything, thought he himself is not subject to anyone's judgment. Therefore, the saint is sent for the Churchs' sake, and it is for the Church to judge whether the saint truly lives and judges everything according to the mind of Christ. As the Church observes the saint's struggles and temptations, his peaceful or violent attacks on the world, his doubts about the life God wants him to lead, and his alternating attraction to the hidden life of solitude and the public life of activity, she must respect the Christian freedom through which grace achieves its particular purposes in his regard. Especially must she respect the model the Christian is following: the Lord who rejoiced and wept, blessed and cursed, triumphed and failed, gave scandal and drew all things to himself.

Two years before his death, already very sick, he was living in a cell made of mats near San Damiano. One morning he said to his companions: "For the glory of God, for my consolation, and the edification of my neighbor, I wish to compose a new 'Praises of the Lord' for his creatures." He sat down, concentrated a minute, then cried out: "Most high, all-powerful, and good Lord! etc." And he composed a melody to these words which he taught his companions. When he was laid low by sickness, he often intoned this canticle and had his companions take it up. He did this until the day of his death. — Legend of Perugia, 42-43, in Omnibus of Sources, pp. 1020-1021.

At the time when he was very sick, the bishop of Assisi excommunicated the podesta. In return the podesta had it announced that every citizen was forbidden to transact any business with the bishop. Francis added the following strophe to his Canticle: "All praise be yours, my Lord, through those who grant pardon for love of you, etc." He then said to his companions: "Go, and in the presence of the bishop, the podesta, and of the entire gathering sing the Canticle of Brother Sun." When everyone had gathered at the place of the cloister of the bishop's palace two brothers began to sing . . . With much tenderness and affection the podesta and the bishop locked arms and embraced each other. — **Legend of Perugia,** 44, in **Ominbus of Sources,** 1022-1023.

CHAPTER VI

OUR HOLY MOTHER THE CHURCH

NOT ONLY HIS own sanctification but also an apostolate with his companions were in the plans of this new "knight of Christ." The group increased in numbers, as Francis wanted it to, but growth brought the necessity of contact and dialogue with the official Church. Once the companions numbered twelve, Francis decided to go to Rome.

The burden of the whole undertaking might weigh on him, but still greater were his hope and confidence. What had he to fear? The life they were leading was inspired by the Gospel, and the Gospel was also the inspiration of the Church. When people asked the brothers, with admiration or alarm, about their external appearance, they replied by dubbing themselves: "Penitents from Assisi." They reminded Christians of Christ, as did other apostolic men of the time, but they spoke as simple teachers of morality, not as preachers of the faith; to act as preachers they would have need both education and authorization. They lived in total poverty, supporting themselves by occasional work and voluntary offerings. They were not a burden to anyone, and on their journeys through Umbria, Tuscany, and the March of Ancona they often spent their nights in sheds, community bake-houses, or on the steps and in the vestibules of churches. They never claimed that only their kind of life was truly Christian, or forced anyone to do as they did. In fact, they showed a childlike reverence for all priests and, in dealing with even the most worldly of them, distinguished the dignity of office from the unworthiness of the person. Unlike Petrus Waldes and others they did not demand personal poverty of the clergy, and neither believed nor said that the Mass and sacraments had lost their meaning and efficacy because of the sinfulness of the priests who celebrated and administered them. They were not proposing a religion purely of the heart, a Church of the Spirit without any outward worship of God. In fact, no one could have been less in a position to take such an approach than Francis in whose eyes everything sensible has an interior dimension, while everything interior sought expression in outward signs. These men believed and felt the Lord to be especially present wherever they found any kind of monument erected in God's honor. At such moments they bowed their heads and said: "We adore you, O Lord Christ, and bless you in all the churches in the world because by your holy cross you have redeemed the world" (Leg. 3 Comp., 37 in Omnibus of Sources, p. 925).

The Pope, however, would not judge by looking at them what kind of men they were, or what light and fire burned in them. They could not themselves describe to him the spirit that moved in their group: how they rose at midnight for prayer, how each admitted his guilt to the others for small failings in charity, how each leaped to the defense of the others when they were threatened on the streets, how they gave alms from the alms they had received, how brother sought the god of brother, and how their lack of possessions brought them a perfect treasure: their poverty of spirit, the perfect freedom of the noble heart. Francis would have to present the Pope with a written expressions of his purposes.

He therefore dictated a Rule in which a minimum of explanation accompanied the sentences he had sought out in the Gospel. One day in early 1210 he said to his eleven companions: "Let us go to our holy Mother the Roman Church and lay before the Supreme Pontiff what our Lord has begun to work through us; so that with his consent and direction we may continue what we have undertaken" (Leg. 3 Comp., 46 in Omnibus of Sources, p. 932). The biographers tell us of a deeply meaningful dream that encouraged Francis at this time. In his dream he was walking along a road when he saw a mighty tree; he drew near it in amazement and suddenly became as tall as the tree so that he could grasp it by the top and easily bend it to the ground.

Under the leadership of Bernard of Quintavalle, whom Francis had appointed for the purpose, they reached Rome. Happily, the bishop of Assisi was in Rome at the time and introduced the brothers to Cardinal Giovanni Colonna. They lived in his house and were able to tell him of the spirit that animated the group. Himself a man of deep piety, he soon realized how deeply serious they were. He had reservations, however, about the severity of their life and advised them to join one of the older Orders. Courteously but firmly Francis rejected the proposal: That was not what he wanted; an inspiration from God had called him to the kind of life he was leading according to the Gospel.

Under the burden of office Innocent III felt like the mythical Atlas who must keep the heavens from collapsing upon the earth. In his slender figure two souls dwelt in an unusual harmony. The man who scorned the world had been appointed to rule over it, and his genius made him at home in both roles. This man, now in his fifties, had for twelve years been ruling a Church in whose flesh the world had become dangerously imbedded. This man of excellent education and

Salomonic judgment, man who liked difficult cases, was melancholy as he contemplated the spots and wrinkles that disfigured Holy Mother Church. Yet he protected her rights with keenness and assurance in his endless dealings with the peoples, the kings, the clergy that was so infected by simony, and the proletariat in the swelling cities as they struggled for their human rights. The varied religious energies that were stirring anywhere among those dedicated to God or among the laity could not but be welcome to him. At the same time, he had to see to it that renewal did not bring innovation. After carefully testing the spirits, he allowed the *Humiliati* of Lombardy, a brotherhood originating among the weavers, to have laymen preach at their Sunday gatherings, and he approved the Order of Catholic Poor men. He was well aware of the countless forms of resistance to papal authority, forms which donned religious or political masks as the situation required; on his journeys and even in his own city of Peter he had seen wild outbreaks of hatred against the papacy. All the more, then, would the Pope welcome any movement in which individuals and groups inspired by the Gospel spontaneously sought whole-hearted collaboration with the Church. Yet to him, as to many of his predecessors, the words of Scripture were applicable: "I know your deeds, your labors, and your patient endurance. I know you cannot tolerate wicked men; you have tested these self-styled apostles who are nothing of the sort, and discovered that they are imposters" (Rev 2:2; cf. I Jn 4:1).

The Cardinal had given the Pope a very favorable report, and Francis and his followers were summoned to the Lateran. The prophet stood before the Pope, the beggar before the sovereign; yet, at the same time, it was one man who scorned the world standing before another. Francis explained his holy purpose and handed the Pope the Rule which now contained necessary points on garb, work and pay, and the acceptance of alms. The Pope expressed both praise and reservations: "My sons, your plan of life seems too hard and rough. We are convinced of your fervor, but We have to consider those who will follow you in the future, and who may find that this path is too harsh" (Leg. 3 Comp., 49 in *Omnibus of Sources*, p. 934). But Francis evidently stuck to his own intentions and the Rule he had written, for the Pope urged him to reflect prayerfully on the whole business and bade him come again.

During these days of high excitement a parable came to Francis' mind. There was a poor but beautiful woman living in a desert. The king of the country discovered her and married her in the hope of having equally beautiful children. When some had been born, he departed and left the mother to live in want with the children. "Do not be downhearted," she told them, "for you are of royal blood." After some years she sent the older sons to court, where the king, struck by their beauty and their resemblance to himself, inquired about their origins. "We are the sons of a poor woman in the desert." The king embraced them and promised to take care of them. "If strangers can eat at my table, how much more you, my lawful sons!" Then he summoned the mother and the other children to his wealthy court. (Cf. Leg. 3 Comp., 50 in *Omnibus of Sources*, pp. 934-935).

The second conversation with the Pope was decisive for both parties and had incalculable historical consequences. In true prophetic style Francis told his parable and explained it. He himself was the poor woman who had been chosen to bear lawful sons to the Lord. The King of kings had assured him that the divine love which cares for strangers and sinners would be even more a source of nourishment for deserving men of the Gospel. The whole attitude of the petitioner filled the Pope with deep confidence in his God-given mission. Therefore, the Pope embraced him and approved the Rule, although only verbally for the time being. The only written statement Francis received were a few words to be set at the head of the Rule, to the effect that the herein described way of life was approved for Francis and his brothers, including those to join the group later on; and that Francis and the head of the community at any given time promised obedience and reverence to Lord Pope Innocent and his successors, while all the other brothers were bound to obey Brother Francis and his successors. At a consistory the Pope renewed the permission already given to Francis and such brothers as he should authorize, to preach morality. At the wish of Cardinal Giovanni all the brothers received the tonsure and thus were incorporated into the ecclesiastical hierarchy, because only as recipients of minor orders could they be allowed to preach in the Church's name.

Thus did Francis bend the top of the tree to himself. After visiting the tombs of the Apostles, the happy companions journeyed back through the Campagna toward the Sabine Hills. Near Orte with its Etruscan underground tombs they spent two weeks resting. Their own interior joy and the peaceful beauty of the landscape were a tempting invitation to remain there and live as hermits intent only on their own salvation. But they took counsel in prayer and were bidden to move onward — toward apostolic work.

CHAPTER VII

FIRST AND SECOND ORDER

IN THE UMBRIAN plain, less than an hour from Assisi, an abandoned shepherd's hut stood, near a leprosarium, on the banks of the "twisting stream" that flowed down from Mt. Subasio, and was therefore called Rivo Torto. This hut was to be the Bethlehem of the new Order. In its narrow confines the "true sons" of the Gospel, these love-inspired servants of Lady Poverty, made their abode. On the posts inside Francis wrote the names of the brothers so that each might have his place. Their daily food, often consisting only of produce they had gotten by begging, was scanty indeed; their rest in the cold nights was short; and the clothing on their shivering bodies was insufficient. To the hard life forced upon them many added further penances, and fell ill of their excesses. Francis forbade the penances, took care of the sick men, and saw to it that they had more nourishing food; he even shared it himself so as to ease their sense of shame.

The work of the brothers consisted partly in caring for the lepers, partly in itinerant preaching. At the bishop's request, Francis climbed into the cathedral pulpit of his native city for the first time; to the crowd, whose attitude had changed since the events in Rome, his words were like "the radiant morning star." Was this man not a prophet, filled with God's

Spirit and sent to rouse them all? This was the man who recently, around Christmas time, did not leave his hut as the Emperor Otto passed by on his way to his coronation, but sent a brother after the procession to remind the Emperor of how empty the world's glory is.

We know hardly any details of the quick spread of the Franciscan movement. We do know that the religious inspiration proper to the movement had increasingly extensive moral and social consequences. An important document of November, 1210, still exists attesting a peaceful agreement in which the upper and lower classes of Assisi — the "big" and "little" people (*maiores* and *minores*) who had long been at odds — united for joint political action, and many burdens were removed from the backs of the oppressed. The name *minores* — lesser, or little, brothers — was already in the Rule Francis had presented to the Pope. Now, the dignity which the name derived from the fraternal spirit in the new Order was communicated to that stratum of the people which bore the same name.

A strengthening of the democratic element in the class struggle may also be inferred from the legends created by the movement. The rapacious wolf of Gubbio which Francis so miraculously tamed undoubtedly signified some greedy feudal lord who under the influence of the new preaching of poverty and peace consented to act with greater moderation. The example and message of these men of the Gospel affected both aristocracy and bourgeoisie, clergy and laity, educated and uneducated.

The hut at Rivo Torto did not shelter the brothers for long. A farmer claimed it for his donkey, and the praying brothers, on this occasion as before, did not resist the evil done them but gave way before the farmer's ugly behavior. There may have been other reasons why Francis left this blessed Bethlehem: the place was too small for the growing brotherhood, and the nearest church was too far away. They therefore left the hut to the lepers and returned to Portiuncula which was to be the Nazareth of the Order.

In 1211 Francis leased Portiuncula from the monks of Subasio for a yearly payment of fish from the nearby little river named the Chiascio. Near the chapel, where the Liturgy of the Hours could now be celebrated with greater recollection, Francis and the brothers built some huts of mud and wickerwork.

New members soon made the Franciscan family a fairly large one. In the traditional accounts some personalities emerge distinctly; these men, usually called the "second generation," reflect the characteristic spirit of the whole group in the variety of their individual differences. Farmer Giovanni at his plough — just where, we do not know — had heard that the well-known man of penance was at the church. He met Francis as the latter was sweeping out the holy place, and immediately wanted to give one of his two oxen to the poor. Francis, sitting with the weeping family at a farewell meal, gave them back their beast but not their father. In contrast to this simple man who imitated his revered master even in the details of outward behavior stands Rufinus, an aristocrat of the Scissi family, and a born monk, serious and laconic. Quite different in turn from Rufinus was the sunny, handsome Brother Masseo with his ready speech, who did not care for much going on pilgrimages since he thought it better to go to the devout men living among us than to the dead saints. There was Brother Juniper, "the Lord's buffoon," who was always ready for some prank, and there was Francis' real confidant, Leo, his confessor and secretary whom he called Brother Lamb but who proved a passionate fighter in the future conflicts within the Order.

For, it was inevitable that there should be times of discord and even of schism concerning the work of the preacher of peace as it became more extensive.

For the time being, however, the heavens were serene and cheerful over the community which Francis controlled with a strict fatherly love that sees clearly and educates wisely. Twice a year, at Pentecost and the feast of St. Michael, all the brothers gathered at Portiuncula for a chapter in which the discipline of the Order was tightened if necessary and individuals were assigned their missions. Francis' words were "fiery and from the heart" as he exhorted, encouraged, and corrected, for, just as he himself submitted to a Guardian expressly appointed to protect him from becoming proud, so he required the other brothers to be obedient in all circumstances, at all times, and in all matters, insofar as conscience and the Rule allowed.

Francis considered it part of a complete evangelical poverty to be fully submissive to authority that was justified by the Gospel and exercised in its name. But the Gospel also sought to prevent the selfish use of authority by superiors when it warned that authority was to be exercised as a form of service in the best interests of the subordinate. Superiors were to be quietly patient; they were "to command in virtue of the vow of obedience as infrequently as possible, and not to act with severity like an officer with his hand on his sword." Obedience was primarily an act of religion, not a following of orders for the sake of discipline; for this reason Francis used to say that a man has not abandoned everything for love of God if he retains the privy purse of his own will. It was inevitable, however, that in the daily reality of a constantly growing society of men there should be tensions and conflicts between leaders and followers. Consequently, far more rules and regulations were needed to keep the whole together and in proper order, than had been required in the early days when the members were few and closely united in spirit. The symbolic dream in which Francis saw himself mastering the great tree that was Pope Innocent was not followed by any other in which he calmed the winds and tempests that would howl through the rapidly growing forest of the Order.

The brothers went ever further afield on their preaching tours, and friends of the movement built hostels where the brothers could put up and avoid incidents that might bring dishonor on the group. Yet "holy poverty" continued to be the secret of their success. Because they had no earthly possessions (says Bonaventure), because they were attached to nothing and feared losing nothing, they were everywhere safe and delivered from the agitation that fear and anxiety bring. They lived free of all inner confusion and could look ahead without worry to the coming day and to any shelter the night might bring.

The sword of separation, one of the sources tell us, was sent upon the earth at this time. In the spirit of that estrangement which, according to the Gospel (Mt 10:34-39), the Lord of God's kingdom effects, the sword cut deeply into the natural relationships that mark the human community. The first woman to tear herself from the family circle was seventeen year old Clare, daughter of an aristocratic house of Assisi, who ran away from her home during the night of Palm Sunday, 1212. At the altar Francis cut off her hair and that of her two companions, bade them don a rough robe, a veil, a rope-belt, and a cloak, and led them to a convent of nuns a half hour away. Soon they moved to another convent, where one of Clare's sisters, despite violent opposition from the family, joined this Order of Poor Women, the Second

Franciscan Order. (Cf. Leg. 3 Comp., 60 in *Omnibus of Sources,* p. 943.)

Once Francis had assigned San Damiano as a convent for this community of women, Clare continued to lead it in strictest poverty for forty years more. She received her second sister and her widowed mother into the community and, despite her strong nature, became the tenderest of mothers to the forty or fifty women who gradually came there to follow the same way of life. Her piety was marked chiefly by her veneration for the Holy Eucharist. Her relationship with Francis grew over the years into a spiritual friendship in which their interior union with each other in the Lord sought more and more a manifestation in outward signs. But Francis was a perfect example to his brothers in the careful distance he always kept from his friend Clare and her circle. His visits were all too infrequent for the women's liking, and, when he did come, he scattered ashes around himself in a kind of charmed circle and began his conversations with the recitation of one of the penitential Psalms. When he once again began to wonder whether he should not lay aside the increasing burden of the Order's business and withdraw to solitude and contemplation, he sought Clare's advice as decisive in the question and received on his knees the messenger's answer bidding him to go on preaching.

The life style of the Poor Clares had, of course, to be accommodated in many respects to the special requirements of women. In the protracted discussions on poverty and possessions there was a conflict between reason with its concern for earthly needs and unconditional trust in him who takes care of the birds and the lilies. As far as Clare herself was concerned, she rejected all offers by the Curia to lighten the burden of poverty. Even after Francis' death she professed with firmness and candor her unalloyed fidelity to the kind of poverty he had wanted. When Pope Gregory IX in personal conversation with her declared himself ready to release her from her vow of poverty since her conscience would not allow her on any other condition to agree to any kind of possessions, her answer was biting in its pointedness: "Holy Father, I want never to be released from following Christ." The Pope granted her the privilege of observing complete poverty, but for the other Poor Clare convents he introduced compromises that no one could think of as mirroring the great-souled rigors of Francis and Clare.

Whether sick or well, Blessed Francis was always solicitous to know and do the will of the Lord. One of the brothers said to him: "Father, know in truth that your sickness is incurable and, according to the doctors, you do not have much longer to live." The Blessed Francis praised the Lord in a great joyful outburst of body and soul. Brother Angelo and Brother Leo arrived and, forcing back their tears, sang the Canticle of Brother Sun. Before the last strophe, they added a few verses on our Sister Death: "All praise be yours, my Lord, through Sister Death . . . Happy those She finds doing your will!" — **Legend of Perugia,** 100, in **Omnibus of Sources,** pp. 1075-1076.

While Francis was living in the episcopal palace of Assisi, seeing that his sickness grew worse from day to day, he had himself carried on a stretcher to St. Mary of the Portiuncula. Since those who were carrying him took the road that went past the hospital, he told them to put the stretcher on the ground so that he would be facing Assisi. Then he raised himself a little and blessed the city of Assisi, saying: "I beg you, Lord Jesus Christ, recall to mind the infinite love that you have shown to this city. May it always remain an abode and residence of those who will know and glorify your blessed and glorious name in the ages to come." **Legend of Perugia**, 98, in **Omnibus of Sources**, pp. 1074-1075.

CHAPTER VIII

INTO THE WHOLE WORLD

THE SOURCES AS a whole have much less to tell us of the interior life of the Saint during the next period than of his external activity. All things considered, these years must have been more painful than the popular memory of the joyful man of God would lead us to think. Moreover, the basic elements of his inner life are difficult to reconcile with one another if one approaches the matter from a purely psychological viewpoint. There was the strong impulse to a world-wide mission, an alternating desire for apostolic work and mystical ecstasy, and a yearning for martyrdom in imitation of Christ. But one thread ran through all: the early Christian "thirst" for the world's last day, when man and Gospel come together in perfect harmony and each fulfills the other.

Let us follow Francis in dry chronicle fashion through seven eventful years.

He was the first founder of an Order to take up the apostolate to the pagans. In 1212 he took ship for Syria, but bad weather defeated his purpose; the ship was driven ashore in Dalmatia, and Francis returned home to preach throughout the countryside amid great rejoicing by the people. In the process he won many new disciples. In the spring of

1213, on a tour through the Romagna, he witnessed a festival of knights and from the walls of a castle spoke to a packed courtyard about the blessings of eternity as a consolation amid earhtly suffering. As a result, a Count in the company invited him to converse on spiritual matters and gave him Mt. Alvernia as a place where he could retire for spiritual recollection. He was active in Spain, probably during the winter of 1213-1214, but illness kept him from going on to his goal, Morocco, and forced him to return home instead. In the year of the great Lateran Council, he wrote from his sickbed his Letter to All the Faithful. It was around this time too that Elias, surnamed "of Cortona," was accepted into the brotherhood; he had earlier been a mattress maker, then a teacher, and finally a notary. This mysterious character, who still continues to be an enigma, would with the passing years cease to be a disciple of Francis and become almost an antagonist of the original Franciscan movement.

In May, 1216, Innocent III came to Perugia in the country of the Saint, in order to establish peace and unity between the naval powers of Venice, Pisa, and Genoa, with a view to a new crusade. He died there on June 16, while Francis was in the city. According to the report of a credible eye-witness, the French Cardinal Jacques de Vitry, the Pope's corpse, robbed of its finery and stripped naked, lay rotting in a church. There was much else to disgust the Frenchman there, but one thing became a source of consolation on this journey:

"Many rich laypeople of both sexes have left all for Christ and abandoned the world. The men are called Friars Minor, and Pope and Cardinals hold them in high respect. They will have nothing to do with worldly affairs but work day and night with passionate zeal to rescue straying souls from the world's snares and to draw these people to themselves. And by God's grace they have in fact reaped a great harvest and won many souls. They live like the early Church, of which we read that "the community of believers were of one heart and one mind." During the day they go into the towns and villages to win people over while at their work, but at night they return to solitude or out of the way places and devote themselves to contemplation. The women, however, live together in special hostels near the towns, accepting nothing from others and living by the work of their hands. It is a source of embarrassment to them that both clergy and laity honor them more than they like.

"The men of this company gather once a year at a specified place, to their own great profit. Their purpose is to rejoice in the Lord and take their meals together. With the advice of good men they draw up and promulgate their holy principles that have been approved by the Lord Pope. Then they disperse for another year through Lombardy, Tuscany, Apulia, and Sicily. . . . I believe the Lord is using these simple, poor people to shame the bishops, who are 'like dumb dogs that know not how to bark," and that through them he will save many souls before the world reaches its end." (Cf. Letter of 1216 in *Omnibus of Sources,* p. 1608.)

Immediately after the death of Innocent III and still at Perugia, the elderly Cardinal Savelli was elected Pope Honorius III. There is a tenacious tradition, open to numerous doubts in view of the historical evidence, that this Pope, at Francis' request, instituted the Portiuncula Indulgence on the occasion of the re-consecration of Santa Maria degli Angeli. In any event, Cardinal-Bishop Ugolino, a nephew of Innocent III, was more important than the new Pope for the progress of the Franciscan movement. In this warm-hearted and pious, but also passionate and ruthless man, the Saint found a friend who, with his sharp eye for Church politics, took a more assertive part in the Saint's work than the latter, the founder, must at times have found agreeable. As a man of religious and social influence, Ugolino took a strong and honorable interest in the new movement, although — or rather, because — his great aim was to draw the movement into a closer relationship with the instituitonal Church. As early as 1217, at Florence, he persuaded Francis, as the latter was on his way to France, to call off his missionary journey. Might not the community stray or collapse during his long absence, since it had only him to restrain it at this time? The community, after all, still lacked solemn written approval, and now the great Lateran Council had forbidden the founding of new orders. Moreover, many of the clergy, especially at the Curia, were opposed to any approval of the movement.

Like it or not, Francis submitted and stayed in the country. The Pentecost Chapter of 1219, one of those "festivals of the poor" during which the brothers lived in huts of woven reeds and grass set up around the chapel, already showed a spirit of planning and effective organization that certainly did not come from the head and heart of the little "stupid fellow" (idiota), as Francis called himself. Nonetheless, the end-result shaped by this new spirit and structured for the good of the visible Church certainly did correspond to the central inspiration of the Saint which he himself interpreted as a divine command.

The Chapter sent brothers to distant regions of the West and to Christians and non-Christians alike. Those sent to Germany met with cruel treatment, while the five sent to the Moors in Spain and Morocco were to suffer martyrdom as early as January, 1220. Immediately after Pentecost, Francis himself, together with Peter of Catania, had set out for

Egypt where the crusader army was engaged in heavy fighting with the Muslims at the mouth of the Nile. The year before, he had sent a group to Syria under the leadership of Brother Elias. When Francis arrived in July, he may have witnessed the carnage that took place around the fortress of Damietta, with both armies committing atrocities. The crusaders, among whom moral depravity had caused frightful ravages, may well have been more open to Francis' preaching after the great battle of August 20 in which they left five thousand dead on the field. At any rate, his preaching was not fruitless: Jacques de Vitry, an eye-witness, tells of four men in his immediate neighborhood who became Friars Minor. But the real aim of the bold apostle was the conversion of the Mohammedans. Despite dangers he managed to reach the Sultan; he was courteously received and sent away with honor, but he was also told that his preaching in the Saracen camp would be allowed only as long as it did not contradict Islamic teaching. His preaching, according to Jacques, lasted only a few days, and the results were meager.

Francis was the first westerner to bring the Christian faith to non-European peoples. He wanted to fulfill the whole Gospel to the letter, including the Lord's command to preach the Gospel to the whole world and to every creature (Mk 16:15). Was an exception to be made for any country, any people, any creature? The message of the rule of the Redeemer God was to be preached to the birds and fishes no less than to the Moors and Saracens. We would radically mistake Francis' personality and work, if we were to think of even a speck of dust in the universe as being outside the reach of his love. We will not understand how loving his heart really was and how it took as its object the whole universe from the stones to man's soul, as long as we do not take into account the mystical union of his whole being with the creating and redeeming Lord as the fiery source of his attitude to reality, his activity, and, not least, his painful destiny. We say too little of him, rather than too much, if we say with his disciple, Thomas of Celano, that he wished to live not for himself alone but for him who hung on the cross and died there for all mankind, and that this wish was the source of his wrestling in prayer, his tirelessness in preaching, and his extravagance in giving an example to others, since in all this he was acting as a collaborator of Christ in carrying out one and the same mission as his Lord.

As the moment of his death drew near, Francis had all the friars who were there called to his side; he spoke to them gently with fatherly affection, consoling them for his death and exhorting them to love God. At last, when all God's mysteries had been accomplished in him, his holy soul was freed from his body and assumed into the abyss of God's glory. At the time of St. Francis death, when it was already dusk, a flock of larks gathered over the building. There they remained, flying about and singing with unusual joy, clearly testifying to the glory of the saint who had so often called upon them to praise God. — Bonaventure, **Major Life,** 14, 5 and 6, in **Omnibus of Sources,** pp. 740-741.

CHAPTER IX

UGOLINO AND THE THIRD ORDER

WHILE FRANCIS WAS in the Holy Land toward the end of 1219, a lay brother who had come after him on his own initiative, brought disturbing news of events within the Order. Without regard for Francis innovations had been introduced in the rule and in the canonical relationship of the Poor Clares to the Holy See. There was no doubt that unauthorized individuals had seized the reins and meant to force development along ways that the founder could only regard as deviations from the original spirit. Rumors at home that Francis lay mortally ill in the East or had already died there favored the innovators. Suffering from an eye-affliction, but unbroken in spirit and master even of his own anger, Francis hastened back to Italy in the company of Peter of Catania, Elias, Caesarius from Germany, and other brothers; they reached Venice at the beginning of March, 1220.

In Bologna he found the community in possession of a house of studies which Peter Stacia, a friar and a learned jurist, had built without authorization. In his indignation Francis ordered everyone, even the sick, to leave the house, and he had not forgiven the guilty man who wanted to destroy his Order, when the man died soon afterwards. This incident was a sign to the returning traveller that the original life

style had already been appreciably altered. But Francis was
to be grieved even more deeply. Sickness had taught the son
of Bernardone the dubious character of human existence;
now, as father and leader of a spiritual family, he experienced
even more intensely the necessity of being among men a man
of the Gospel and among Christians a complete follower of
Christ.

"The leader of a great and complex army, the shepherd of
an extensive and widely scattered flock" — that was what
Francis had now become, and the growth of his work only
increased his distress. For, along with those who were truly
called came many without real vocations: lax brothers, vaga-
bonds, and parasitic adventurers of the kind Francis angrily
called "Brother Fly." Even a friend of the movement, Jacques
de Vitry, noted the breakdown in a letter of 1220 from
Damietta and regarded the Order as a public danger because
monks wandered about "two by two" in an undisciplined
way. In the ecclesiastical world of France the introduction of
the Order was opposed on the grounds of a distrust which
the Pope countered in a strongly worded letter of recom-
mendation. The same Pope, Honorius III, in a Bull of September 22, 1220, prescribed that in the future any entrant
must pass a year in probation and that vows made at the
close of the novitiate year were irrevocable.

This important edict, which created a close resemblance
between the mystical band of brothers and the great Orders
with a long history behind them was preceded by an important meeting of Francis with the Pope at Viterbo, a meeting
Francis had sought. At the meeting he asked for and received
Cardinal-Bishop Ugolino as protector of the Friars Minor.
Perhaps Francis realized that law and precept must hold together what love could no longer unite. We do not know the
feelings with which he entrusted his work, now threatened

from within, to the protection of the Curia, but certainly this unreservedly devoted son of the Church was also a sharp-eyed judge of the Church's prelates whose lives were so alien to the gospel. We have evidence of this in the passionate sermon he preached extempore before Pope and Cardinals; he took as his text a verse of a Psalm on scandal and disgrace, and completely forgot about the ideas Ugolino had suggested to him. (Cf. Cel. I, 73 (p. 290); II, 25 (p. 383); Leg. 3 Comp., 64 (p. 948) — pp. in parentheses in *Omnibus of Sources.*)

The things Francis honored from the depths of his being he wanted to see visible in the pure lives of those who held positions of respect. He did see them in Ugolino. Ugolino, however, while honoring the man and the saint in Francis, also saw it as his task now and for the future to put these sources of new strength at the service of the entire Church Universal. This shrewd Roman, a fifty-year old man of great experience, was like an older friend who puts his arm around the shoulder of the younger and tries to bring the latter around to his way of thinking by invoking his own authority in a gentle, encouraging fashion. The relationship of Ugolino and Francis in the subsequent years was marked by a conflict between two human beings but, underneath that, by a conflict of forces. Questions like these suggest themselves in this context: Will culture and the gospel tolerate each other? Must not the mystic of unalloyed imitation of Christ come into conflict with any form of existence in the world, even that of the ecclesial community, and must not the world come into conflict with him if it goes its own proper way? The gospel rule of God never quite comes into existence, never takes on palpable form: Does not this very impossibility make of it the true incomparable treasure that all history is seeking?

Francis' attitude to the ecclesiastical protector of his work
was one both of obedience and of resistance. He obeyed
Ugolino as a priest and authorized man of the Church; he
resisted him as one who was a threat to a purely divine mission that was anchored in the gospel. The conflict — and
it was a conflict for Ugolino no less than for Francis — came
to the surface initially in regard to cultivating knowledge and
possessing books. Only the deep religious spirit of both men
can make it understandable that such matters should have
become the occasion for a lengthy and absorbing struggle. As
a matter of fact, the conflict, even as seen from Francis' side,
had and still has no satisfactory resolution. For, if scholarship
and research represent a danger to poverty of spirit and if
the collecting and possessing of books is incompatible with
complete poverty of external property, on the other hand,
the active life of the Order, directed as it is to winning souls,
especially through preaching in defense of the faith, requires
intellectual education and formation.

The saint himself had a genuine reverence for learned men
and liked to have them around him from the beginning. He
himself appointed the highly educated Portuguese, Anthony
of Padua, as the Order's first teacher, and, in naive respect
for the written word, he preserved pagan writings from destruction because even they might contain something of value,
in enunciating which the human spirit could direct its innate
powers to the Lord. But in this age of flourishing university
life Francis saw a great deal of pride abroad with its resultant
division of minds. As a result, any considerations of the
value of learning were outweighed, in his eyes, by a deep-
seated suspicion that intellectual activity could only harm the
pure simplicity and devotion which are the inner sources of
true wisdom. Therefore, though he loved educated men, he
barred the way to education for himself and his followers and

condemned the tree whose noblest fruits he really wanted very much. To cover up or explain away this division within his own mind in this regard (and it is a division he was not alone in experiencing) does not do justice to him or to the kingdom of God, that most real of realities which nonetheless cannot be made fully real in our finite world.

At the Pentecost Chapter of 1220 stormy tensions that had been irresistibly building up burst out into the open. The brotherhood that Francis had joined in marriage to Lady Poverty saw disorder and an alien spirit ravaging its ranks. There was a cry for a more stable constitution and for the freedom to obtain at least a modest education, such as was already accepted in the older Orders. Ugolino undertook to win the founder over to the wishes — really the demands — of the "ministers." Without answering, and trembling in his agitation, Francis took the Cardinal's hand and led him out before the assembly. Then, in a passionate outburst, he defended the mission he had received from God to be a fool in this world and to lead others in the path of wisdom. His excited state reduced everyone to silence and dismay, but very soon the Order had entered on the course from which Francis sought to keep it. Among the reasons justifying this choice was the example of the Dominican Order, which was becoming widespread at this very same time, for it already had a clear constitution and had made study its primary aim. Cautiously, but with a clear knowledge of where they were going, Ugolino and the Curia guided the threatened Franciscan ship toward its future. On board that ship was the builder, and no one was more distressed than he. Within his lifetime the Friars Minor would proceed in droves to the Universities of Bologna, Paris, and Oxford.

At the Autumn Chapter of this same year (1220), Francis resigned his office as head of the Order and handed it over to Peter of Catania, one of the original disciples. When the latter died shortly after, in early 1221, he was succeeded by Brother Elias whose gifts and worldly outlook would lead him so far from the spirit of his master that the Order would finally expel him. If the harshest witnesses against him are to be believed, we cannot simply dismiss as groundless the comparison of his role in the Christ-like life and activity of the saint with that of Judas.

Elias was thus the one who presided over the great "Chapter of Mats" during the week of Pentecost, 1221, at which thousands of the friars gathered. Francis preached on the Psalm verse: "Blessed be the Lord, my God, who strengthens my hands for battle." Speaking and praying, advising and commanding, he finally became exhausted. At the end of the meeting, too tired to speak any more, he sat at Elias' feet, plucked at the latter's cowl, and gave him the necessary cues for sending friars to the German mission.

In this same year, 1221, occurred an event of incalculable importance: the promulgation of a rule of life for the Third Order. With this action the evangelical movement spread widely and entered deeply into the social and political life of the time. The way had long been prepared by the desire of countless laypeople, especially those already united in various religious fraternities, to share in the spirit of the Poor Man of Assisi, without having to change their state of life or abandon family and profession. Democratic opposition to the feudal order and religious opposition to the parasitic encroachments of the world on the Church also played a part in the rapid multiplication of tertiaries. The movement was a peaceful revolution but one that nonetheless deeply affected the structures of society.

According to all indications, Ugolino's influence on the origin and development of the Third Order was extensive, but the person and example of the new "fool for Christ" were the source of the movement and the reason for its powerful yet peaceful spread. Francis, who had sacrificed everything and wanted nothing but that the rule of God, with its eight beatitudes, should lay hold of men's hearts, lived to see crowds of people from the oppressed masses streaming to him. He and his followers carried to the people the banner of a Church whose ideal was poverty, and saw it become a power in public life, without any appeal to hatred and rebellion. Townspeople and farmers, soldiers and artisans, menials and servant girls followed that banner. Francis, with his strong sense of the order among the classes of society, did not incite the lower against the higher, but held them to the payment of their taxes to the landowners and reconciled the towns to their feudal lords and bondsmen to their masters, even when the latter were nothing but knightly brigands. At the same time, however, the prohibition against bearing weapons and taking the knightly oath that bound the Brothers and Sisters of Penance (the early name of the Third Order) was a deadly blow to the heart of feudalism. The feudal lords realized the turn things were taking and spoke of rebellion, but the townspeople with their Guelf sympathies saw the developments as a religious sanction of their thirst for freedom.

Holy men are never forgiven for manifesting the shocking seriousness of the Gospel by the excessive demands they make on themselves. Their success or at least their efforts in carrying out, as far as grace and their human strength allows, the demands God makes of men in the religion of Jesus Christ, their passionate struggle to become as perfect as the heavenly Father within the limits possible to a creature — all this gives the whole existence of the saints (few of them so obviously as St. Francis) the appearance of something the ordinary man can only judge alien, exaggerated, and even a threat to society and the very concept of man. The immediate impressions produced by a saint, his otherness, his rejection of the everyday judgments of men, his disregard of social forms and ties, often too the disturbing bodily manifestations of a soul on fire: these make him a burden to those around him and an object of suspicion to the foolish, and draw down on him (the more so, the greater the saint) curses and persecution from the fellow-Christians closest to him.

But the roaring flames of a conflagration, while hard to endure from close up as the wood is being consumed and the fire draws ever new intensity from it, bring a comforting warmth to those at a distance. The saint, after all, does not live only for his own age or for the places his feet tread, and even if he wanted to hide his lamp under a basket, it would soon burn right through. Whether or not he intends to, he will sooner or later affect his more distant contemporaries and later generations. Silently they wait for him — to thrust his weight against the gates of hell, to wash in the Lamb's blood the robes of the sinners of an age, and, by his own utter forgetfulness of self, to renew the divine nobility of the human soul. Even where men do not admit to such expectations or where the superman of the Gospel is dragged down and reviled, the yearning for "the race that seeks for him, that seeks the face of the God of Jacob" (Ps 24:6) spontaneously comes to life over and over again. How could it be otherwise, since the natural man, when left to himself, cannot live up even to his own nature but necessarily sinks beneath it?

When sorrow makes life a burden, and all the more in times of general upheaval, even the average man looks for the just one who comes as dew from heaven. The words and actions, the endurance and sacrifices of the saint may be beyond the reach of many, but the latter realize that he exists for their sake and has risked everything for love of God. Men do not forgive his success, but much less do they forgive him for being broken and shattered in his effort to reach an impossible goal. In God's sight he becomes a sacrificial victim for all mankind. He gives strength even to the weaker brethren and fills with his life blood the cups of those who are not his peers but nonetheless, amid the constraints of an ordinary life, hunger and thirst after justice.

Thus the Third Order of St. Francis, despite its ups and downs and even the shadows that mark its history, has had a broad and profound influence on the west. Among the great names that occur in its pages are Louis IX of France, Elizabeth of Thüringen, Dante, Columbus, Michelangelo, and Galvani. Imitation or the admiring desire for imitation has been enkindled in many tertiaries across the centuries by the spirit of St. Francis, the conquistador of God's kingdom. It was a special kind of spirit, a response of the Christian heart such as was unknown before or since. The words of the Apostle apply even to the heaven of the saints: Star differs from star.

When, with the sons carrying their father, they came to the place where Francis had himself first planted the religion and order of holy virgins and poor ladies, they placed him in the church of San Damiano, where these same daughters whom he had won for the Lord dwelt. There they paused, and behold the Lady Clare came with the rest of her daughters to see their father who would no longer speak to them. Divided between sorrow and joy, they kissed his most radiant hands, adorned with the most precious gems and shining pearls; and when he had been taken away, the door was closed to them which will hardly again be opened for such great sorrow. — Celano, **First Life**, 10, 116 and 117, in **Omnibus of Sources**, pp. 330-331.

CHAPTER X

THE PASSING OF FRANCIS

THE VITAL FLAME leaped up once more as the conqueror for Christ made bold plans. But this man marked by grace and unable now to walk made no more lengthy journeys on his donkey. It was a further burden to him that the curious sought opportunities to see the wound-marks; he evaded them as best he could and kept questioners at a distance, probably with brusque words: Mind your own business! Almost fully blind now, but with his inner eye all the more alert to God's presence in all things, he lay, after the incident at Alvernia, in a dark hut of reeds that Sister Clare had built for him at San Damiano. Mice drove him almost crazy, but one night, after calling out to God, he was told that he would certainly reach happiness in paradise. The next morning he awoke in utter happiness of spirit and composed his Canticle of Brother Sun, a hymn of praise to the revelation of God's glory and love in creation. In the very depths of poverty he had reached a state of supreme adoration.

At the urging of others he put himself into the hands of the doctors a year before his death. At Fonte Colombo, a hermitage in Rieti Valley, he underwent an attempted cure that was torture: the doctors opened the veins between ear and eye and cauterized them. As the hot iron was drawn from the flames, he prayed the element, for love of him who had created them both: "My brother fire, the Most High created you strong, beautiful, and useful. Be kind to me in this hour, be courteous." And he endured the treatment without showing any pain. (Cf. Cel. II, 166 in *Omnibus of Sources*, p. 496.)

He spent the winter of 1226 in the home of the Bishop of Rieti and then in the spring went to a doctor at Siena. After a violent hemorrhage, he wanted to return from there to his own country. An armed escort came out to meet him, a guarantee that his native city would have possession of his dead body. He arrived at Assisi mortally ill and accepted shelter in the Bishop's home. In September the doctor told him he must die. At this he extended his arms and said: "Welcome, Brother Death!" He bade his companions, Brother Angelo and Brother Leo, to sing him the Canticle of Brother Sun. When they had finished, he dictated a new ending, the praise of Brother Death.

Then he asked to be taken to Portiuncula, and they carried him there on a litter, one fine September day. At the half-way point he had them turn the litter, and he blessed Assisi, which he could no longer see: "I beg you, Lord Jesus Christ, Father of mercies, do not pay heed to our ingratitude, but remember always the immense love you have shown this city. May it always be the dwelling place of men who in ages to come will truly know you and glorify your blessed name."

He lived a few days longer, A noble Roman lady, long his friend, had a sure foreboding of his death and came with a great retinue to visit him. Francis in turn had been wanting her to bring him once more the almond cakes he loved.

After a night of great pain he exhorted and blessed the assembled friars. He also blessed bread and gave it to them while the Holy Thursday Gospel about the Lord washing his disciples' feet was being read aloud.

Then, in a hut, he had himself stripped, lying naked on the bare earth, he asked for a much-mended habit as a final alms. He wanted to hear the Canticle of Brother Sun sung over and over again.

The next evening he sang with a clear voice the Psalm: "With a loud voice I cry out to the Lord" (Psalm 142). Then he died; it was after sundown on October 3.

The next day, a Sunday, all Assisi came in the early morning to escort the body. The procession detoured through San Damiano, past the weeping Sisters, past the crucifix from which he had received his call.

Ugolino, who became Pope Gregory IX, canonized his friend only two years later.

The further we get from the times of this Saint, the more difficult it is for us to understand his actions in the light of the motives that really shaped his unique life. This is even, and indeed especially, true of his relationship to other men. It is easy enough, of course, and quite legitimate to sum up that relationship in the word love or charity (*caritas*), but everything then depends on grasping the true and full meaning of this word. Thus, Francis, was the humblest of men, and yet it is impossible to overlook in him the dignity of a man accustomed to rule or the bold freedom with which he insisted on carrying out, in himself and in his followers, the command he had received to serve the Lord. In other words, his love of men derives its norm and measure from above, not from the upsurge of sentiment, still less from a sense of brotherhood based on human solidarity. His love for men does not have its ground in man as such, nor his love for the poor in the poor as such. At the same time, however, even the Christian concept of charity does not express the essence of his basic relationship to men.

Francis loved because he was loved. God had gazed upon

him with love, and he in turn became a channel bringing to every human being and indeed to every creature this primal force that sustains all things in being and that had become visible to him in the love-inspired sacrifice of the Son of God and swept him out of himself. A comparison with sexual love will give some distant understanding of Francis to anyone in whom a blissful marital love flows over into generosity to all around him. This natural manifestation of eros, and indeed the outgoing nature of all goodness, and its power — like that of the sun that causes leaf and flower to turn to it — of drawing what is distant into communion with itself: all this is an image of that infinitely higher relationship in which the love (*caritas*) of God, that loving mercy that is the source of creation and redemption, calls man's power of love into play, so that ("for the love of God," as Francis used to say) he may bind himself and all that makes up his life to the love of the first Lover, God. Love of men — what could be more obvious in such a view of the world!

Even when the heart is choked by debris and the spirit has gone astray and vice has mutilated the traits of God's image in the soul, God's love for man continues to be the measure of man's love for others. Thus, man's love does not need to be stirred to life by compassion, for it had and still has its ground in a man's very being as image of the First Lover, to whom neither divine nor human writings attribute compassion. Compassion is a spontaneous movement of the psyche, whereas mercy is a free act of the spirit that sets the psyche too in motion.

Love, or charity, in this proper sense of the word (the agape of the New Testament) is not directed immediately to man, in order to satisfy God who requires it. It is directed first to God. But if one is to love God with all one's strength, one must inevitably share his love for men. Since, however, man is not God but a creature and since his sense of creature-liness is the root of his religious attitude to God, his love, however intimately linked to God's, will always be aware of sharing the common condition of the creature before God. Therefore, love's first and chief concern in this world that is necessarily infected with evil is not the fight against suffering and distress, but dedication to God as the source of good for all beings. We would radically misunderstand the great lover Francis became if we took his selfless life of poverty to be a way of alleviating social ills.

Francis left the rich in peace unless they wanted to become his disciples; then he insisted on a complete renunciation of property and even forbade new friars to leave their possessions to their own families. He never said a word against the idea or the legitimacy of property, nor did he stir up the poor against the rich. He simply gave rich and poor alike an example of the indescribable wealth that extreme poverty freely accepted brings. He was utterly unconcerned with the welfare of men in purely humane terms. The whole force of his nature and of a personality that in the last analysis had a demonic quality about it was focused on an interior work of love, although the latter had revolutionary effects in the external order as well. He had nothing and wanted nothing, yet how much he could have given! He lacked not only the formation but the will to be a social reformer; how else, then, was he to attack the serious social problems of his day, except with the power of his grace-filled heart? Yet, just because his heart was on fire with seraphic love of what is beyond time, his hands inevitably opened wide in the effort to make God's love a reality here on earth, at least in symbolic actions that were touchingly small by human standards.

This poverty chosen for love of the poor Savior of all creatures was Francis' great gift to mankind. He showed men that, and how, all things human are to be approached with the conviction that things eternal are real. An unsophisticated religious spirit enabled him to live a truth which Thomas Aquinas, the greatest mind of the other mendicant Order, was to express in theoretical terms not long after Francis' death. "If a person is less than another in the order of being, it is a greater and better thing for him to be united to that higher being than to supply what is wanting in an inferior. Therefore, since man has God as his superior, the love that unites him to God is a more excellent thing than the mercy by which he meets the needs of his neighbor" (St. Thomas Aquinas, *Summa theologiae,* IIa-IIae, qu. 30, art. 4). According to this principle, even the greatest works of mercy that flow from Christian charity as men usually understand the latter cannot be regarded as the supreme expression and fulfillment of the Christian religion; much less so, if such works of mercy spring purely from the community's sense of self-preservation.

Of Francis his first biographer says that, with all the religious ardor of his soul (*viscera pietatis*), he followed in the footsteps of the poor Christ and became the servant of the poor, but that in giving alms he sought to strengthen men's souls rather than simply to help them in a material way (*carnis subsidia*). "His gaze was always fixed on the face of his Christ; he was always seeking out the Man of Sorrows who was well acquainted with distress." But the saint could not make even his own followers into men exactly like himself. He said prophetically that the austere would relax their vigilance and tepidity would become widespread. Even before he died, his own Order saw the rise of a critical attitude toward the original demands of poverty as Francis conceived it, and an acceptance of the doubts voiced by the official Church.

Was there not a danger, after all, in the decision to scorn all things earthly and transient so that the human spirit might be able freely to unite itself with the eternal Lord and God? The history of the medieval poverty movements is a story both of men reaching the freedom of St. Paul's "using the world as though they used it not" and of men destroying themselves through cynicism and even nihilism. We may not simply shrug off the objections of those who not only opposed the poverty fever that swept across the scene like an epidemic, and the language born of social resentment and envy, but were suspicious also of the mendicant Orders and even strongly resisted the very principle of poverty. For, this great struggle brought to light the deeper problem of being and having in a world in which time and eternity are rivals. One of these opponents, Guillaume de Saint Amour, a theologian at the University of Paris, was indeed condemned, thirty years after Francis' death, for such views as this: "Begging is dangerous because men who live by begging become flatterers, slanderers, liars, and thieves, and will have naught to do with true justice." But we must remember too that Thomas Aquinas, an opponent of Guillaume and an enlightened defender of the mendicant Orders, wrote as follows: "Those who wish to live virtuously must avoid, it would seem, both excessive wealth and begging, because both extremes are occasions of sin. Great wealth is an occasion for pride; begging is an occasion for stealing, lying, and even perjury. Christ, of course, being incapable of sin, . . . had no need to avoid these extremes. — Not all begging, however, is an occasion for stealing and perjury, but only begging that is unwillingly undertaken, so that to escape it a man will steal and perjure himself. Voluntary poverty is not open to this danger. This is the kind of poverty Christ chose. . . . If a man is poor out of necessity, his humility deserves no great praise, but if he is poor by his own choice, as Christ was, his poverty is proof of very great humility" (St. Thomas Aquinas, *Summa theologiae,* IIIa, qu. 40, art. 3, ad 1 et 3).

In clinging steadfastly to extreme poverty and requiring his followers to do the same, Francis waged a very peaceful war on mammon and its servants. It is difficult, of course, to show in detail the blessings and peace he brought to individual hearts and to society at large. We can readily maintain, however, that he looked on all charitable and humane activity as an imitation and repayment of God's love which became incarnate in Christ, and that he did what he could to teach this lesson to the world through his self-sacrifice with its depths of suffering and joy. The primal love that is the origin of all creation as the sun is of the day is to be encountered, in its full reality, only in another world. Here on earth, therefore, where that love is absent and yet not absent, Francis could weep as one in exile, but, because he also glimpsed the hidden shores of eternity in the distance, he could also be as happy as a child.

He was completely unconcerned with what men call culture, because to those who seek God's kingdom all those other things will be given into the bargain. The only community he was concerned with was the communion of saints, and it was in order to serve it that he founded his austere brotherhood under the eyes of the crucified Christ. He nourished the brotherhood — and indeed far more than it — with a love that praises and shouts from the housetops and gives itself without reserve, a love that is foreknown and therefore knows what is at sake when the human creature takes its destiny seriously. God may give you all riches, but no riches can give him to you. A man preserves the coin he holds in a closed fist, but the soul he does not give away — is lost.

CHAPTER XI

THE SERAPHIC SAINT

IN HIS LAST years, the truth that "in weakness power reaches perfection" was proved in the saint. The accounts do not give us clear insight into his interior state, but the facts they do provide enable us to draw some sure inferences. Pain of body and soul mingled with a joy that kept bursting into song. The shadows around him became more impenetrable for him, but the inner light was clearer and sweeter. Some words of the Apostle about a community that had found joy in giving even amid its own distress probably express best the mysterious depths of Francis' two-sided relationship to heaven and to earth; applied to an individual, the text would read: "In the midst of severe trial his overflowing joy and deep poverty have produced an abundant generosity" (2 Cor 8:2).

When, after lively discussion, the rule had been given its definitive form in the winter of 1223, Francis, tormented by demons, went on foot to the friars who were living in Rieti Valley. Amid the wild Sabine Hills, in a forest lit by the torches of the crowds that had gathered, and in the midst of manger, ox, and ass, Francis celebrated the feast of Christmas with his brothers. He preached, but was so overcome by the love God had showed in his coming among men, that he could not speak the name of Jesus. As he moved from one place to another, the only apostolate left to him was that of example and written exhortation; a great deal had still to be said that was not in the rule. Eyes growing blinder, worn out by many illnesses, and sleeping little (he slept now sitting, now resting half-awake on wood or stone), he went about, tormented by evil visions and consoled by heavenly ones, or else he lay in dark huts, "not so much praying as becoming himself a prayer" (Cel. II, 95 in *Omnibus of Sources,* p. 95).

There can be no doubt that in Francis' life, as is that of other saints, there was a connection between holiness and illness. There are divergent views about which of the two is cause and which effect, and each views has good arguments on its side. But only stupidity, or something worse, will conclude from the connection that, since holiness is so often accompanied by a breakdown in health, it must itself be an illness. In such a view it is as though health were the only human value (whereas the best Greeks required beauty and goodness!). Among the great figures of history we can count the very healthy much more quickly than those who were frail and sickly and perhaps even defective in some way or subject to attacks.

In regard to these people, and especially the saints, a third judgment seems the best: The total makeup of these people was subject to a law according to which the ultimate goal they wanted, and which it was intended they should attain, could be reached only at great cost to the material side of their nature. The words of a German mystic express the point well with regard to the world of nature and the world of the created person: "If a being is to become what it is not as yet, it must cease to be what it is." Thus there is a negation, but for the sake of something positive; the grain of wheat must split open and lose itself if it is to bring forth much fruit.

Earlier times, unlike later ages with their denunciation of the saints, did not fail to recognize a redemptive meaning for the negative, for illness, and even for psychic disturbances. This was reason enough for the men of earlier times to accept and embrace illness with patient resignation and even with joy. To seek out illness is and has always been to enter on a false path, and many have had occasion to regret their excessive asceticism as a self-willed attack on the Creator's right to dispose of his creature; even Francis at least warned others against this course. But this proved nothing against the generally accepted principle, based on experience, which led Hildegard of Bingen to say: "God usually does not make his dwelling in a healthy body."

In the eyes of the believing Christian, after all, man's earthly existence is not the ultimate value for him; rather, like the rest of creation, this existence is undergoing change toward a condition in which it will correspond perfectly to the model the Creator has for it. This whole process, which we, whose vision is limited to time, cannot fully comprehend, presupposes a power at work that is antecedent and superior to the law of movement and of change for better or for worse that is innate in all natural things. One aspect of the process is that there is a healthy (in the highest sense) way of being ill.

Especially does man become aware that the word "nature" does not adequately describe his being. This realization turns his attention, if he is a Christian, to a world of freely acting causes that do not derive from nature's determinisms and that can work on him, and become active in and with him, in such a way that he sees his nature not only as accessible to these causes but as a changeable material which they can shape. He believes in grace; he speaks of the superhuman; amid the existence he calls life he receives from faith the concept and reality of a life in relation to which the first life is as opportunity is to fulfillment. The Christian, too, hears the command: "Become what you are," the call to ultimate self-realization. But when eternal life visits natural life, the visit may involve an act of violence, a physical upheaval. In this case, illness, while an evil, is an evil for the sake of a good; it is the sign of a transformation in which the new cannot come into existence without the sacrifice of the old.

The science of man's physical nature is therefore quite justified in applying the names of various illness to unusual or abnormal states in the lives of the saints, but it is not for it judge that these phenomena, because pathological, are simply meaningless. Even on the long road that ended in the Garden of Olives and on Calvary there were dismaying signs of "abnormality." Christ began his career as a man tempted by diabolic visions, and it was only after the cry of abandonment by God that his end came with the quiet commendation of himself into his Father's hands. In between lay his great healing work as he "cured the people of every disease and illness" (Mt 4:23). But Christ himself, to whom all sufferers came, gave the impression, in moments when his powers were taxed to their utmost, of being mad or possessed; his nearest relatives could not recognize him in this state and said that he had gone mad. As liberator of men from evil, he spent himself to the point of exhaustion where he wanted nothing but to rest, yet even at such moments he would appear to his disciples when they were in danger, and would let them lay hold of him.

His messengers and saints resemble him, within the limits of their powers and the grace given them, in his consuming passion for the rule of God. Now, the life-histories of these men and women very frequently manifest the presence of pathological conditions, but we must take into account the fact that very many of these people are to be regarded as victims of their own mistakes and that if they had not been ill their holiness would have been much more tolerable and attractive to others. But, when due allowance has been made for this, there remains an objective connection between holiness and illness, and the opinions of the pathologist must not be allowed to lead the theologian astray in his own proper sphere. The pathologist offers a judgment, as is right and fair, on the state of a man's natural constitution; the theologian sees the same man as part of a greater and more comprehensive reality that is not limited to the world of nature. If, then — as is the case today — medical research sees a positive value in one of the evils of illness, namely pain, not only because it signals danger (the ancients spoke of pain as the barking watchdog of health), but also because in many cases it contributes to the healing process, then the question inevitably arises, especially for the Christian, whether the whole of the evil that is sickness may not have a purpose and a meaning. May it not warn us or help us to a cure which leads to life on this side or the other side of the grave?

The last years of the saint were a time of suffering that the historian cannot easily comprehend, but at the same time they were, to the Christian viewer a time of rather evident transfiguration. Ever since the moment of his radical turning to the sacred humanity of the eternal Christ, Francis had given himself wholly to collaborating in the ongoing work of redemption. We know of no time when he wavered or was perplexed on this point: if his suffering and pain intensified, so did his mystically intimate union with the glorious Passion of the Servant of God who gradually changed and at last wholly transformed this man of poverty with his radical openness. Francis' transformation into the likeness of his model began with his change of outlook in youth. With metanoia came metamorphosis. In this context we should not hesitate to use the vocabulary of "transformation" as the Scripture uses it. Francis was one of those who, "gazing on the Lord's glory with unveiled faces, are being transformed from glory to glory into his very image by the Lord who is the Spirit" (2 Cor 3:18).

Hardship within and without only led him more fully into the communion of love to which he was chosen and called. Neither the distress which love itself caused him nor the rankling pain, finding vent at times in outbursts of anger, at the distortion of his ideal, the influx of worldly concerns into the Order, and the desire of some friars for rank could plunge his soul into gloom. Others might succumb to "the Babylonian sickness," that darkness of soul in which a man, experiencing the absence of God, turns back for consolation to the Babylon he had left behind; Francis was kept safe by the light and music within him. "At times he would take a piece of wood in his left hand and, with the right, draw another stick across it as though it were a violin. From the wood he drew melodies that voiced the sorrow in his heart. Meanwhile, to the dumb music only he could hear, his body would sway to and fro. Whenever he did this, the tears ran down his face, until at last he threw violin and bow and finally himself to the ground and was transported within his soul."

From his sick bed Francis sent the Pentecost Chapter of 1224 a letter with admonitions and a confession of his sins. In the summer he went with a few close companions to the mountain wilderness of Alvernia which he had long loved, in order to undertake his customary forty-day fast in honor of Michael the Archangel. Suffering from an eye affliction, his body full of pain, and his soul galled by the realization that the Lord's commission would not be carried out in all its demanding austerity, he climbed the mountain and rejoiced when the birds came and settled on his shoulders, knees, and hands as the party sat under an oak to rest.

He began his prayers and penance on the Feast of the Assumption. Brother Leo, the person closest to him during these days and weeks, witnessed extraordinary occurrences involving the saint's person and actions: ecstasies, levitations, light phenomena. Brother Leo is the single authority on which all the accounts of the saint's wounding by the seraph ultimately depend.

It was around sunrise on September 14, the Feast of the Exaltation of the Holy Cross, that the lonely wooded mountain became both Golgotha and Tabor for this follower of Jesus. Sudden ecstasy brought a vision: he saw above him a man resembling a six-winged seraph who, with arms outstretched and feet joined, was nailed to a cross; two of his wings met above his head, two supported him in flight, and two covered his whole body. — When the saint came to himself after this blissful yet terrifying vision, he found the five wounds of the crucified seraph on his own body.

While still deeply moved by his experience, Francis wrote on a sheet of parchment for Brother Leo a hymn of jubilant adoration and with it a short blessing of Leo himself. The latter added a few sentences to the manuscript later on. In this most ancient of written testimonies to the stigmatization Leo writes as follows: "And the hand of the Lord was laid upon him; after the vision and speech of the Seraph and the impression of the stigmata of Christ in his body, he made and wrote with his own hand the *Praises* written on the other side of this sheet, giving thanks to the Lord for the benefits conferred upon him" (*Omnibus of Sources,* p. 124). — The many discussions of the matter leave no room for doubting the authenticity of this parchment with its faded letters.

The origins of all that is most important in history, and

especially in the history of salvation, are usually obscure. What emerges to the public eye and exerts a gradual influence is already the effect of a cause that is for the most part obscure even to the agent of the action, to say nothing of others. If Francis were asked about the origin of his stigmata, natural reserve would probably have prevented him from saying anything at all about it; but if he were to attempt an answer, he would be perplexed about what to say, surely far more perplexed than later generations which, down to our own day have tirelessly argued the whether and the how. And if he had indeed told us what went on in that ecstasy, we would have to counter with the words of the great Spanish lady of Avila as she looked critically at her description of her own mystical experiences: "How can I, as a person in an ordinary state of mind, pass a valid judgment on the experience of the different person I was in ecstasy?"

There is reliable testimony from any quarters that Francis actually bore the stigmata. In addition, persons from outside the Order gave sworn testimony in 1226 about what they had themselves seen during the lifetime of the saint and after his death. These various statements are the basis for the exact description of the wounds that was given at that time; it is a description with which the one given two years later by Thomas of Celano, Francis' disciple and biographer, is in full agreement. Brother Leo himself, the first eyewitness, is the source of the shorter description in the Legend of the Three Companions. Leo tells us that though the man of God sought to hide "God's gift," it became known to at least his closest associates. "After his death, however, all the brothers who were present saw clearly that his body bore the wounds of Christ in hands and feet. In those wounds there appeared to be nails, but these were formed by Francis' own flesh which had taken on the shape and color of iron nails. The right side over the ribs looked as though it had been pierced by a lance with a plain and obvious wound, covered with a red scar with crimson edges, and during blessed Francis' lifetime blood often flowed from this wound" (Leg. 3 Comp. no. 70, in *Omnibus of Sources,* pp. 952-953).

The emotion of love, which like all the other emotions affects man's body, has always been compared to a wound, but as far as we know it has never been seen actually to wound the flesh. In Francis, however, the "wound of love" did become a "wound in the flesh"; what he saw while in a state of rapture laid hold of his material nature and left its image therein. In the recollection of men, that had never happened before. When it happened thereafter to hundreds of others, holy and unholy, people attempting to explain these later occurrences could fall back on the original stigmatization and claim that it led to an imitative repetition by men and women in hysterical states. There was no such model, however, for the stigmatization of Francis himself. Psychiatrists may be able to offer no working model of explanation except hysteria and its attendant phenomena; we, at any rate, must take other causes into account. Some have simply denied the whole occurrence; others have spoken of wounds secretly self-inflicted. Both "explanations," however, are untenable, because since Francis' time others have borne the stigmata and these have arisen spontaneously, without help from outside.

As far as Francis' own stigmatization is concerned, then, it is an enigma, and we may safely predict that it will remain an enigma, since it becomes meaningful only as part of that realm of mystery in which Francis' person, work, and destiny were situated. To say this is, of course, to forego all explanation, and the very fact of its inexplicability becomes an evident pointer to the mystery. But what else can we say except that in a nature so uncommonly sensitive to exterior and interior events the hidden stigmatization of the crucified spiritual soul left its mark on the corporeal nature as well? Such a statement as that, however, does not really bring us any closer to an understanding of the mystery. The mystery is there and must simply be accepted.

To anyone long familiar with our saint nothing can be more distressing than discussion of his stigmatization in the only terms available to the natural sciences; nothing more gratifying than the reserve and brevity of Brother Leo's original account; nothing more enlightening than theological meditation on the saint's "suffering in Christ" by grace of the "God who is wonderful in his saints"; nothing more moving than the simple words of the Church's prayer concerning this man whose following of his Redeemer was sealed in such an inconceivable way: "Lord Jesus Christ, to set our hearts on fire with love of you in a world grown cold, you renewed the sacred marks of your suffering in the flesh of St. Francis . . ."

CHAPTER XII

THE SPIRIT OF FRANCIS

IF WE TRY to capture this "spirit" of Francis in a single word, the best word, the one that gets at the very root of the matter, is *nobility*. The word points not only to the natural quality of this man who showed such sensitive concern for others (*cortesia, gentilezza*), but to the whole manner in which he understood and approached all of reality: God and every single creature. We may discover in him any virtue we choose, but shaping them all is the noble mind, the greatness of heart that manifested itself in his attitude to God, the world, and man, and in his dealings with every being, from the highest to the lowest.

The longer and more deeply we contemplate the innermost motivating forces of this personality, the more dubious become the words we use in trying to explain him; this has to be admitted right at the beginning. Not only is he, like every individual, something that cannot be captured in words (*individuum ineffabile*). More than this, the element of the holy in him, the sacred that thrusts its way into the temporal world as something alien and demanding, as though it came from outside or even from another world, and shatters the accepted framework of things — that element of the holy, which comes both as a gentle breeze and as storm and lightning, leaves us in darkness as to what nature and grace or grace as mistress of nature have set in motion. But since the saint also has a particular human constitution and a corresponding historical mission, we are both permitted and required to take careful note of the natural elements in him. Many questions will remain unanswered, but here the saint himself shares our embarrassment, for when he is asked about the origin of what is transpiring in him, he will attribute his inadequacies to himself and everything else to the irresistible power of grace.

The feeling of dependence on a supreme personal reality which is itself unconditioned while it conditions everything else remained with the young gentleman of Assisi after he recovered from his illness; it was the abiding fruit of the dreams of feudal glory which he had cherished at the dawn of his manhood. In his soul the kind of allegiance which his age idealized was carried over and applied to the intimate relationship of the human being to the Lord of time and eternity. It was Francis' mission to give an eternal validity to a passing earthly relationship and thus to save history from the transitoriness of all historical reality by linking it to its ultimate meaning, the kingdom of God.

For Francis, religion was a relationship between aristocrats. It knows nothing of a demeaning "I give, so that you may give in return." The Lord is the good Lord: the Lord, but good; good, but the Lord. "Taste and see how good the Lord is. . . . Fear the Lord" (Ps 34:9-10). Truly he is the Lord, because he freely creates all things and rules all for the good of those ruled. Such a Lord deserves a service inspired by an equal nobility. To give that service is the mission of the spiritual and therefore free creature, who is also to give it in the name of the lower creatures put at his disposal. It is precisely man's dignity that obliges him to serve God's honor; and this service is the perfect fulfillment of his dignity. In his exhortation to all the friars, the saint writes: "Try to realize the dignity God has conferred upon you. He created and formed your body in the image of his beloved Son, and your soul in his own likeness" (Admonitions, V in *Omnibus of Sources*, p. 80). Thus, the very nature of man, since it is like God, should determine him to give himself and all he has to God. Because we have received everything and have it only on loan, we must eliminate the element of "property" from our lives and activity at every level. In all things we are but stewards, and man's ultimate nobility is to "render" unto the Lord what he has received.

To render unto the Lord in the completest possible way: we will find that this inner impulse marks every aspect of Francis that is well attested. He follows the impulse himself, he requires it of his followers, and he requires it of all human stewardship. The idea itself, of course, is not a new one. But a newness and uniqueness does attach to the dedication and power with which this individual believes that he has fittingly responded to the inconceivably noble divine feudal Lord only if he practices the complete self-renunciation proper to a vassal. The crucifix-centered piety of the age (involving a mystical exchange with the Son of God on the freely chosen wood of sacrificial abasement) and especially Francis' own firm conviction of a command that came expressly from the Crucified One also contribute to make this "renderer unto to the Lord" feel obligated to a reparation or satisfaction that can in fact never be truly satisfactory because the goodness of the Lord is infinite.

Once Francis had experienced the Love from heaven as deeply as he did (by reaason of his natural capacity for prodigal love, apart from any other consideration), he saw himself put in the distressing position of all lovers who have found that the measure of love is to love without measure. Love does not become a source of distress because this or that individual aims higher than his strength will enable him to reach. No: love is of itself a torment because the "ever more intensely," the "ever more deeply," is grounded in the very nature of love. By its nature love is never satisfied, and therefore it consumes the one whom it sets on fire. So too, without itself being a virtue in the strict sense of the word (because a virtue must always be on guard against turning into its opposite), love is stronger than death. For, in its urge to go ever further it pays no heed to death and knows that it will not have reached its goal and completion, no matter when or how death may come. The only image that befits love is the fire that consumes the very wood out of which it emerges and from which it reaches out to lay hold on all around it.

"Seraphic and all on fire," the saint in his passion for God sees every created thing as an image or sign of God. Every creature comes forth from God and therefore is worthy of honor; it seeks to return to its home in him who is the goal of every inclination found in nature. In saying this, we are already expressing Francis' relationship to creatures and to man's use of creatures within a given culture. In both areas he has been misunderstood, especially by generations that have lost sight of or rejected the Cross. It would be a complete mistake to applaud when this man of tender heart clasps an animal to his breast or builds nests for birds, as though he were loving nature simply as nature and with a love that regards nature as the ultimate and best and only reality. This was not at all the case with Francis; "nature" in this sense familiar to later ages was unknown to him.

We must note that this man of sensitive feeling for the dumb or vocal, lifeless or living signs of the Creator was also horrified by the mutual destruction that is so often the fate of these creatures. Like other men who take the kingdom of God by violence, he was often tormented by demons who attacked even his body; but, again like them, he paid the dark realm back in its own coin, as nature possessed of such great capacity for love cannot help doing. Thus he had a tender affection for the animal that he thought of as especially set apart by the Lamb of Golgotha, but he was overwhelmed by a demonic, passionate anger against another beast that was no less the product of God's creative hand. A sow had bitten a lamb to death in the stable during the night, and in the morning the saint cursed it with such destructive force that the innocently guilty slayer died after a painful sickness and withered away in the monastery ditch, a piece of carrion no other animal would eat.

This occurrence is rendered credible to us precisely because it lies like a dark shadow amid the many charming stories. It shows the saint caught up in the same vortex of unified disunity which mysteriously characterizes all created reality when we try to comprehend it. One might attempt to reduce the element of irrationality and contradiction in this curse-hurling disciple of the Lamb of God by claiming that Francis was only avenging innocence in a symbolic way. But have we any answer save silence to the question of where the guilt is that is to be expiated? In this story a beast that can claim no merit is the victim of a beast that cannot be blamed, and a human being falls into a passion in his zeal for justice against injustice! This man loves nature and this man hates nature — and acts as representative of the opposing forces that are inherent in all of creation. He is a lamb to the lamb, a destroyer to its destroyer, and in his heart gives rein to the natural urge that says yes to what is charming and no to what is ugly. This man who curses and in whom the power of love and the power of anger intensify each other thus shows himself to be fully at one with nature which is divided within itself. Love for a creature rouses his wrath at its destroyer to the point of destroying the latter in turn, even though it is only a creature like the other.

Francis' heartfelt sympathy for creatures is part of his devotion to their creator. In every work of the Father eternal love wells up, the same eternal love that called him, Bernardone's son, to the light and visited him with grace. Sun, fire, water, the earth he walks on make the presence of the one Lord sensible to him. In that presence all the things this Lord created are so bound into a familial unity that the tender names of Brother and Sister, addressed to flower and brook and the singing denizens of the air, are but a natural echo of the one Love from which at every moment and in every place all created things flow forth. In his responsive love that seeks to give all things back to the Lord Francis protects and cares for creatures: carrying the worm away from the dangers of the trodden path; honoring in the drops of water that fall as he washes his hands the pure element that is itself clean and cleanses all else; and challenging the sun to vie in song with the human heart and its psalmody.

As for culture — that whole relationship of man's searching, sculpting, shaping spirit to his world — what is it but a "rendering unto the Lord" (*restitutio ad dominum*)? Yet, was there any place for it in the mind and heart of Francis? He preached as harsh a contempt for the world as any desert monk or preacher ever had, and his longing to be emptied of himself was pushed to a dangerous extreme, as though man and human nature must suffer shipwreck on God in order to satisfy God. Perhaps it was this danger, a kind of religious existential compulsion which lays hold of the mystic and sometimes the moralist (Tolstoi, for one), that made the Church bar the path he had followed, since the Franciscan

Order could not possibly contain nothing but Francises, and, besides, a crowd of Francises would have shaken all social structures, including the Church insofar as it is a society.

People speak of the tragedy of this saint, but we must remember that for the Church too it was a tragedy, and indeed an even more dramatic one than for Francis. The Church too feels its great saints to be a burden — and to that statement only a stupid mind will react with shallow mockery. The law of preservation until a final day which it is not in the Church's power to decree is at odds with another law of her being: the law of change. Both are imposed by the gospel: to stand and abide like a building, to grow and develop like a plant. The former requires unyielding fidelity to the word that will not pass away even if heaven and earth pass away; the latter requires freedom for the Spirit to blow where he will, though we do not know whence or whither. Since the Church is the Church of the incarnate God, she is divine for the sake of men. And since she is the Church of men moving toward God no less than the Church of God coming to men, she must respect God's action in and through the individual as being the action of the same Holy Spirit she knows to be leading her and bringing her to her completion.

One manifestation of the Spirit thus guiding the Church and bringing her to completion is that chosen men who follow Christ speak to the Church on behalf of their Lord, even while they listen to the Church because of the same Lord. The answer the Church gives them through the mouth of her men in authority has for its ultimate criterion the truth she has received through revelation and tradition. Thus her answer has the status of a divine judgment. But even during the very lifetime of a religious man who is moved to his depths and in turn moves his world, the Church may already have prudential reasons, based on concern for the whole body (often pitifully human reasons!), for stripping a saint of his weapons or at least blunting the point and edge of his sword. In such circumstances, the Church gives the impression that it does not want its word, which at bottom is the gospel word, to be taken very seriously. Or do we have here more than a mere impression? Does the tragedy of the saint who, like the Lord, comes to his own and is not received correspond to the equally real tragedy of the Church which must take into account the world it is to rescue and preserve, no less than the kingdom that is not of this world? Can she allow man and mankind to perish through contempt for the world and through the action of the world-scorners who appeal to the same gospel that gives her the task of communicating to the world the fruits of the Redeemer's work? In this world-age of the Word made flesh can the prophet's declaration ever cease to be true: that God does not wish the human spirit he has made to perish from before his face? Does the kingdom of heaven not exist for the world's sake and the leaven for the sake of the dough, and is not the Church the woman of the parable who mixes in the yeast so that the whole mass may be leavened?

We are confronted here by the mystery of the kingdom of God, by a division, manifested in time, that will not be eliminated by denial of its existence. In the vortex of this struggle between the opposing forces of time and eternity, of this kingdom that is not of this world yet exists for this world, Francis of Assisi, and the Church with him, was caught up. He drove himself to complete self-sacrifice for the Lord and the kingdom, and he did so in childlike allegiance to the Church. The Church listened to him, honored him, promoted his work; but when the work seemed to be turning dangerous for the whole body, she took it into her own control and mixed it like yeast in her three measures of dough.

Francis fulfilled the gospel, but so did the Church. He did the perfect thing that is not required of all because "for man it is impossible." The Church supported him and promoted his work to the point at which she considered she must stand up for what is normally possible to men and suffices "to possess everlasting life." In the same way, Jesus himself did not do away with the requirement addressed to all, that they enter life by keeping the commandments, for the sake of a superhuman requirement that is possible only "for God" (cf. Mt 19:23-26). That which he required of his disciples in the narrower sense of the word — a perfect following of the messenger of God's kingdom — goes beyond the command given to the many, without either obliging the latter to the same perfection or playing down their place in the kingdom.

We might attribute the hidden tragic conflict between Francis and the Church to the abiding discord between individual and society. If we look more deeply, however, we will find that it arises out of the existential situation of man as such, for man, once he has become aware of the demands inherent in his innate likeness to God, also becomes aware that he cannot satisfy these demands. Augustine spoke for countless others when he said: "I grow fearful because I am unlike him; my heart takes fire because I am like him." Under the pressure of that first feeling, Francis the penitent, the sufferer, the man of sacrifice, sought to annihilate himself. Under the influence of the second, Francis the heir to divine life, the man filled with love and song, celebrated his own existence and that of all other things as a great festival.

He experienced these feelings not in alternation — up today, down tomorrow — but simultaneously, and jubilant poverty was the expression that embraced both heights and depths and did justice to both the penury and the wealth that is man's. A poverty that was not satisfied to remain merely interior, since everything divine must take bodily shape, enabled him to accept the world ever anew as a pure gift, as though it were only at that moment emerging in pristine splendor from the merciful Creator who summons it out of nothingness. Standing in the empty neighborhood of nothingness he was filled with happy amazement that anything at all existed, and the smallest thing, the slightest sign of the love that wills reality to be, roused in him an overwhelming response of gratitude, praise, and love. It is as Meister Eckhart says of him: "The poorer in spirit a man is, the more he is detached and regards all things as naught; the poorer in spirit he is, the more do all things belong to him. Once he has realized that having, in the ordinary sense of possessing, is a danger to his being, once he has measured the depth of the words 'I am' as a Christian ought to be able to say them, less and less becomes for him more and more. The more fully he has sacrificed the temporal ego to the eternal self, the more truly it can be said of him: 'I have been crucified with Christ, and the life I live now is not my own; Christ is living in me.' "